Practically Christian
Applying James Today

Phillip A. Ross

Practically Christian—Applying James Today

ISBN: 978-0-6151-7667-3
Edition: 4.15.2014

Published by
Pilgrim Platform
149 E. Spring St.
Marietta, Ohio 45750
www.pilgrim-platform.org

Printed in the United States of America

In the hope of restoration

BOOKS BY PHILLIP A. ROSS

The Work At Zion—A Reckoning, Two-volume set, 1996.

Practically Christian—Applying James Today, 2006.

The Wisdom of Jesus Christ in the Book of Proverbs, 2006.

Marking God's Word—Understanding Jesus, 2006.

Acts of Faith—Kingdom Advancement, 2007.

Informal Christianity—Refining Christ's Church, 2007.

Engagement—Establishing Relationship in Christ, 1996, 2008.

It's About Time!—The Time Is Now, 2008.

The Big Ten—A Study of the Ten Commandments, 2001, 2008.

Arsy Varsy—Reclaiming The Gospel in First Corinthians, 2008.

Varsy Arsy—Proclaiming The Gospel in Second Corinthians, 2009.

Colossians—Christos Singularis, 2010.

Rock Mountain Creed—The Sermon on the Mount, 2011.

The True Mystery of the Mystical Presence, 2011.

Peter's Vision of Christ's Purpose in First Peter, 2011.

Peter's Vision of The End in Second Peter, 2012.

The Religious History of Nineteenth Century Marietta, Thomas Jefferson Summers, 1903, 2012 (editor).

Conflict of Ages—The Great Debate of the Moral Relations of God and Man, Edward Beecher, D. D., 1853, 2012 (editor).

Concord Of Ages—The Individual And Organic Harmony Of God And Man, Edward Beecher, D. D., 1860, 2013 (editor).

Ephesians—Recovering the Vision of a Sustainable Church in Christ, 2014.

TABLE OF CONTENTS

ACKNOWLEDGMENTS

IT IS THE RARE BOOK THAT is the product of only one person. This is not that rare book, for I am indebted to many people for their gracious help.

First, I have fed upon two classic Protestant Reformers in my study of James, John Calvin and Matthew Henry. My indebtedness to them is foundational.

I have also leaned upon my friend Gordon Keddie. Americans are not likely to know of Gordon. He's a Scot who was serving a church in State College, Pennsylvania, when I was in that area. Keddie is better known across the British Commonwealth. His book on James, *The Practical Christian*, (Evangelical Press, England, 1989) has provided great insights and challenges. I am indebted to him for his work. Unfortunately, you won't find his books at your local Christian bookstore. But in these days when the Internet is all the rage, his work can be found through an Internet search, or through Evangelical Press.

I also want to thank the people of Putnam Congregational Church who first heard these chapters as a sermon series on James. Since its first preaching I have refined some of this material to make it appeal to a wider audience, though for the most part is remains much as it was first heard.

When publishing became more of a reality I asked various friends for their consideration and comments of the manuscript, and made various adjustments to it related to their comments. That has been an enriching and helpful process.

Rev. David Brand (Charlottesville, Virginia), Dr. John Gilmore (retired, Cincinnati), Dr. Jonathan Gold (Wheeling, West Virginia), Dr. James E. Martin (State College, Pennsylvania), and my friend Angela Longheinrich have each and all contributed to this work. Thank you all for your patience and understanding, for your time and careful reading, for your friendship and thoughtfulness. Thanks also to my wife, Stephanie, who continues to love and comfort me in my ministry in spite of the difficulties. Thanks also to Dr. Douglas Vickers, who recommended that I make the effort to publish my work.

INTRODUCTION

JAMES WAS WRITTEN TO CORRECT A church that was going astray in the early years of Christianity. From James we learn that the gospel is intensely personal, that it is not just a matter of signing a pledge or joining an institution.

The gospel, James reminded his readers, is a practical way of life. And where the actual living of that way of life is *not* demonstrated in the lives of Christians, the Holy Spirit must be presumed to be absent and the faithfulness of such people called into question. The gospel is not just a head belief, nor a heart-felt experience. It is primarily a way of life. Initiated through the grace of God alone, the gospel is not the gospel apart from its actual, behavioral manifestation in the lives of believers (James 2:14).

This book seeks to shine the light of Scripture into the darkened recesses of the contemporary church by shining the light of James into the hearts of its contemporary readers. This is an intensely personal work in the sense that it attempts to get at issues that few people (or preachers) are willing to talk about, but are essential for the gospel to take root in our lives.

As such, the following pages will provide a critique of the contemporary church from a biblical perspective, that of James. Many beliefs and practices of contemporary Christians and their churches will be found to be short of the biblical mark. As James has been grist for my mill, so I offer this as grist for yours.

Rather than a straight-forward commentary on James I have put together various thoughts and tangents that have been inspired by James in the midst of ministry. My objective is to help people see that James is applicable today in the same way that it was when it was written.

I pray that the Lord will use my efforts as He sees fit, and that you will see the gospel anew and our contemporary biblical challenge afresh.

Though the original edition was first preached in 1995, and published in 2001, it still has application. Indeed, the application is not mine but belongs to Scripture itself. Thus, it will always have application. I pray that it will be useful for you.

Phillip A. Ross
Marietta, Ohio

SURVIVING TEMPTATION

My brethren, count it all joy when you fall into various trials,
knowing that the testing of your faith produces patience. But let
patience have its perfect work, that you may be perfect and complete,
lacking nothing.   —James 1:2-4

A young Christian was asked what she did when she was tempted. "When Satan knocks at the door of my heart," she replied, "I simply ask Jesus to answer it." She went on to explain that when Jesus answers the knock of the tempter, Satan says, "Oh, excuse me. I seem to have make a mistake. I was looking for someone else," and leaves.

In faithfulness God dwells in the hearts of believers. When you are living a life of faith, the living Word takes command of your life by means of the written Word. The faithful find themselves wanting to live according to the dictates of the Bible. So, when we let Jesus answer temptation on our behalf, we experience the joy of victory over Satan and his minions and their myriad temptations. Yet we cannot believe that this victory over temptation is a once and for all victory. Temptation continues to sell its wares every day. So, no matter how many victories we have, we will never have enough strength in and of ourselves to stand against Satan. Rather, every time temptation knocks, we must ask Jesus to answer the door.

The Greek word for *trials* is the same as the word for *temptation* in the Lord's Prayer, "and lead us not into *temptation*" (Matthew 6:13). Can there be joy in trials and temptations as James suggests? According to Scripture there not only can be, but there definitely is. The idea of joy in the midst of trials is found, for instance, in the Beatitudes.

"Blessed are you when they revile and persecute you, and say all kinds of evil against you falsely for My sake. Rejoice and be exceedingly glad, for great is your reward in heaven, for so they persecuted the prophets who were before you" (Matthew 5:11-12).

Christianity is nothing if not joy in the midst of struggle and gladness in spite of personal persecution. The Jews have always been a despised people. The nations of the world have always hated and warred against Israel. Like the Jews, the Christians whom Jesus addressed in the flesh would also be rejected by the world because of their faith—some even by their own families. The stories of Jesus[1] and of Paul[2] testify to the rejection of the gospel by the world.

We know that this situation—the hatred of God's people by the world—was not unique to the Jews and Christians of the First Century. Rather, the world has always hated God and His people—and it still does. In all of history there has never been a time of greater Christian persecution (more individual Christians being persecuted) than during the Twentieth Century. More Christians have been martyred during the Twentieth Century than during any other period in history. Why?[3] Perhaps because modernity has produced the most materialistic (worldly) culture ever known, and the gospel of Christ has always cut across the grain of worldly, materialistic values.

This means that Christians of all people should feel the tension and stress that is generated by living a Christian life in a fallen world, especially today. Faithful Christians of any stripe, living in a worldly culture, will be at odds with that culture. They will be out of step with society. Genuine Christians will not simply be out of date, not into the latest fads, but they will stand outside of the flow of fads and popular culture altogether. Christians will struggle to not get caught up in worldliness.

However, this is not an endorsement of a retreat-minded, ghettoized, and separated Christian subculture. It's not that we need to join

---

1   For more on the rejection of Jesus, see *Marking God's Word—Understanding Jesus*, by Phillip A. Ross, Pilgrim Platform Books, 2007, Marietta, OH.

2   The story of the rejection of the gospel continues through the adventures of Paul in the book of Acts. See *Acts of Faith—Kingdom Advancement*, by Phillip A. Ross, Pilgrim Platform Books, 2007, Marietta, OH.

3   See *Humanity: A Moral History of the Twentieth Century,* Jonathan Glover, Yale University Press, 2000.

the Amish or found some other Utopian commune. Not at all! Rather, it is a call to change the worldly culture in which we live with gospel of Jesus Christ. We are not to retreat from the world. We are to overcome it, or better yet, to overtake it, to overwhelm it with a host of ordinary Christians endeavoring to live ordinary Christian lives. We are to starve the fires of worldliness—greed, passion, lust, gossip, fear, etc.—with a lack of interest in sin.

In The Culture But Not Of It

The Greek word *ekklesia*, which is translated *church*, means "called out ones." Christians are not to shun or spurn the culture in which they live because they are to live *in* it. But neither are they to be captive to culture. They are to be in control of the grip that culture has upon them and their families. Christians are to be *in* the world, but not *of* it (John 17:15), to live in it but not to find their interest or identity in it. Our interest and identity are to be found in Christ.

Jesus said it this way, praying to the Lord for His people,

> "While I was with them in the world, I kept them in Your name. Those whom You gave Me I have kept; and none of them is lost except the son of perdition, that the Scripture might be fulfilled. But now I come to You, and these things I speak in the world, that they may have My joy fulfilled in themselves. I have given them Your word; and the world has hated them because they are not of the world, just as I am not of the world" (John 17:12-14).

Christians are to live *in* the world, but not live *as* the world lives. We are to live in the midst of sin, materialism and worldly values—because there is no other choice, but we are not to share those values. Christians are to march to the beat of a different drummer. Christ sets the pace among the faithful, not the world—not television, not Wall Street, not fashion, not popular literature, not success, not institutional growth, not Christian romance novels or end times fiction, but Christ, and Christ alone—and that according to Scripture alone.

In a sense it might be easier to be *in* the world but not *of* the world if you lived as a missionary in a foreign culture than it is to do so in one's own culture. At least as a missionary it would be clear that your own particular values and customs were supposed to be different from the people around you. But because we in America are in the habit of thinking that we live in a Christian nation or society we are tempted daily to believe that every innovation coming down the pike has God's blessing. Too many modern Christians are more likely to christen the values of their society rather than stand against them, more likely to succumb to the peer pressure that calls people into conformity to God-lessness than to resist it. Too many people in our churches have never dealt with the clear commands discipleship in, for instance, Matthew 5:30 or Matthew 18:8. Most contemporary churches do not understand or ask for such discipleship commitment.

The application of this insight of James is to "count it all joy when you fall into various trials" (v. 2). We are called to apply spiritual joy to our trials and temptations. But how? How does that happen? It seems so contrary to our normal experience.

Biblical application always begins with belief. We must actually believe the gospel. We must trust it and live by it because it is faith and belief that are to be applied to our lives, not Bible stories. Like paint applied to our homes to beautify and protect them from a hostile environment, so faith and Christian belief are applied to our lives for beauty and protection. But applying Christianity to real life situations is much more difficult and complex than painting a house. Where paint is applied to the outside, Christianity must be applied on the inside before it ever shows on the outside. Right belief works hand-in-hand with right understanding.

JOY IN TRIALS

To understand how joy can be applied to personal trials we need to understand the difference between *happiness* and *joy*. Christ calls us to joy, not to mere happiness. It is not that Christ calls us to unhappiness. Not at all! Christ is not opposed to happiness. In fact, Christ provides the only real, lasting happiness that is actually possible. Yet we must understand that human happiness is a by-product of Christ's love for His people and His obedience to God. It is not the main concern of Christianity but is a derivative of it.

The word *happiness* is derived from the root *hap*.[4] From *hap* we also get the words *happen* and *happenstance*. Happiness is essentially an appropriate response to present circumstances. A truly happy person does not wear a plastic smile. Happiness is an appropriate response to

---

4   *Oxford English Dictionary*, Oxford University Press, 1971.

one's current circumstances. Crying at a funeral is an appropriate response. Fear in the face of danger is appropriate. Consequently, true happiness involves a range of emotions that are evoked by various circumstances. In genuine happiness there is a balance of joy and sorrow that is appropriately determined by one's circumstances. The downside of happiness is that people who are merely happy live at the mercy of their circumstances. Happiness is like a ship at sea, it is subject to the waves and winds of its current situation. And here is where the joy of Christ takes precedence over happiness.

Joy is the application of Christ's love in all circumstances, no matter what the situation, no matter what is happening. Christians can always lean on the love of Christ, calling to mind the eternal joy of salvation. Christians can call upon Christ's love, trust Christ's commitment, trust the fact that His obedience and subsequent death on the cross has indeed paid the price for the sin of every believer. No matter what anyone may have done (in the way of personal sin), no matter what anyone throws at us (in the way of trials or temptations), we can trust in the love and obedience of Christ. He loves His people and defends the faithful, no matter what. His sacrifice has provided for the salvation of every believer. Here is real joy! Here is joy that is not subject to the conditions and circumstances of the world.

Under the pain and stress of persecution, Christ's love and obedience are triumphant. Under the awkwardness of being called a nerd, or the stress of going against what may be popular, Christ's love and obedience promise and produce true and lasting joy. You see, joy is not mere happiness. Joy does not include being tossed to and fro by worldly circumstances. Joy is claiming personal happiness in Christ, no matter what! Joy is holding fast to the eternal happiness, promised and delivered by Christ, in spite of our circumstances.

Joy doesn't depend upon our circumstances. Joy does not adapt itself to circumstances, but to Christ. Joy claims the happiness of eternal salvation in Christ regardless of worldly and temporary circumstances. Christian joy is applied to life. No matter what life throws at God's people, the joy of the Lord is anchored on the rock of Christ. The Rock holds fast in the midst of life's storms. That's joy!

WHY ARE CHRISTIANS SO DOUR?

London is known for its high culture and worldly satisfactions. A wealthy man residing in a fashionable part of London was consumed with the pleasures and entertainment of high society, eating and drinking at the right places, being seen by the right people.

Encountering a woman he knew to be a Christian at a shop one day he asked, "Why is it that religious people are always trying to rob the world of its pleasures? I enjoy life, and I can't see why they should be forever trying to take away from me what little pleasure this short life affords."

He pretended not so much to ask the question, as to ponder out loud in her presence.

"You are terribly wrong," the aging woman responded, "if that is what you think. Christians don't want people to give up pleasure or happiness. Rather, we encourage people to receive a greater pleasure, and a greater happiness than anything they have ever known."

The rest of the day he could not stop thinking about the idea of receiving a greater pleasure than high society provided. After all, he prided himself on having attained the greatest pleasures known to humanity. About a year later, he ran into the woman again, and admitted that his life was miserable.

"It is an empty, meaningless round of chasing temporary satisfactions that always end, leaving me less and less satisfied," he reported.

He asked her about the joy she had told him about, and inquired about what he must do to receive the greater satisfaction of Christ that she had spoken about.

She took out her Bible and showed him the promises of God and the forgiveness of the Savior. She gave him her Bible, and soon he found the pardon, acceptance, and that joy that he had never known before. It was just as she had said.

The greatest pleasures the world can offer—even the most tempting enticements of Satan himself—cannot hold a candle to the eternal joy of knowing Christ. Do you know what I'm talking about? Are you familiar with that kind of Joy?

Growing Deeper

My brethren, count it all joy when you fall into various trials,
knowing that the testing of your faith produces patience. But let
patience have its perfect work, that you may be perfect and complete,
lacking nothing. —James 1:2-4

There is more to mine from these first few verses. The reason that Christians are to count it joy when they fall into various trials is not that they like pain and difficulty. Christians are not called to be masochists. We are not to confuse pain and joy, suffering and pleasure. Rather, we are to look to the end of our lives, and to the fulfillment of God's purpose.

There is a God-given sequence in James—trial, joy, patience, maturity, and perfection. The order is significant because it is God's order. If it were up to us, we would put joy at the end of the process, as a reward for good behavior. But God does not put it at the end. God makes joy the engine of patience and the means of perseverance. Christians persevere patiently because to do so gives them joy.

We should also note that this sequence does not work for everyone, but only for the regenerate, only for God's people, only for those who actually live faithfully. It works only for those who are born again, only for those who are actually led by the Holy Spirit through the Word of God. It only works for faithful Christians because it is the Holy Spirit Himself who provides each element of the sequence.

Without the active leading of the Holy Spirit, trials do not produce joy, nor does joy produce perseverance, etc. Pharaoh was not led by the Holy Spirit, but was subjected to Godly trials by the plagues called upon Egypt by Moses. And rather than joy, Pharaoh's trials produced hardness

7

of heart. Pharaoh refused to be led by God's Spirit. The key or beginning of spiritual growth is regeneration, which results in submission to the Lord.

THE CHANGLESS CHANGE

At one time the Great North Road in India ran through the Punjab and the United Provinces. One side of the road was soft dirt for camels, the other side was paved for automobiles. In the rainy season the soft dirt turned to mud. A man was walking to Calcutta in the rainy season. Being inexperienced with highways, he found himself walking in the mud. The going was slow and his feet grew heavy as they caked with the Punjab mud.

One day he met a man going the other way who told him that walking was easier on the paved side of the road.

The mud-caked man moved over to the pavement and in a very short time he proclaimed that his life had been changed. He felt lighter, like a new man. He had great joy in his new situation.

Down the road, he met another man. This one had a Bible and was going his way. As they walked this man talked about the truth of God in Scripture. After some days of traveling together, the man with the Bible said, "I have two questions for you. First, where were you going when you were walking in the mud?"

"Calcutta," he answered.

"And where are you going now that you are on the pavement?"

"I'm still going to Calcutta," the man answered.

"Then your life has not changed," said the man with the Bible. "Only the ease of your travel. Your destination remains the same. The change you experienced has not helped you, but will only speed you to your godless destination. What you need is a new life, a new goal and new purpose—a new destination. Only then will your life be truly changed."

The moral of the story is that God is not here to help us do what *we* want, or to help us go where *we* want to go, or to get what *we* want to get. Rather, we are here to serve God, to do what *He* wants. There is a world of difference between using God to help us do what we are already doing, and doing what God wants us to do.

TRIALS DO NOT PRODUCE JOY

The Bible tells us that we should meet trials with joy, and joy with patience. The joy is not so much a product of the trials, as if suffering causes joy. Suffering doesn't cause joy. Rather, the joy is given by the Spirit as we discover that we are caught up in God's salvation. No one enjoys suffering. Rather, Christians enjoy knowing that the final end of their suffering will be the perfection that comes with spending eternity in Christ. And so God's people put up with their suffering because Scripture teaches that suffering itself is part of God's ordained process of spiritual growth. As pain is part and parcel of birth, so suffering is part and parcel of spiritual maturity.

Joy in the Lord balances the trials and afflictions that come from living a Christian life in a fallen world. We suffer affliction and temptation, yes, but the joy of Christ is greater. Notice also that joy serves as a counterbalance to patience. There is no joy in simply having patience, but again patience in the Lord brings the joy of Christ, the satisfaction of salvation. Having passed through various trials, Christians find joy in the knowledge that God has reached out and by His grace alone He has saved them.

But just as suffering can cause us to err by pulling us down too low, so joy can cause us to err by lifting us up too high. When we focus too narrowly on our own suffering, when we are caught up in the struggles that suffering brings, we can lose sight of Christ and of His joy. Similarly, we can overindulge the joy we find in Christ and loose sight of His ultimate purpose. Both are errors of self-centeredness.

Christians are not to merely endure the trials of this world by scowl and determination, but to keep themselves from being overwhelmed by the world's difficulties by keeping our eyes on Jesus. We are to meet every trial with joy. Neither are Christians to set their faces in a perpetual smile that betrays the pride of self-satisfaction. Just as the faithful are not to be overly gloomy, they are not to be overly joyous either. Too much gloom masks the joy of life, and too much joy obscures the chastening of the Lord. Both the joy of Christ and the pain of His chastening are real, and both must be reckoned with.

NOT GLOOM BUT PATIENCE

According to James, the counter balance for joy is not gloom and sadness, but patience—perseverance. As odd as it might seem to the world, Christians are to meet adversity with joy, and joy with patience. When Christians over-indulge in emotional and spiritual enthusiasm because of their joy in Christ, the Spirit calls them to patience to keep them from spiritual pride and self-centeredness. Just as joy in the face of trial is God's remedy for the struggles of the faithful, so patience in the face of overwhelming joy is God's remedy for inflated emotionalism. Christians are not called to go bonkers for Jesus, but are called to an ordinary and responsible life in the midst of their present circumstances. God always seems to be working to balance the excessive emotions and passions—the highs and lows—of His people.

Why does God do this? Because people are at risk of being led astray by the flesh and its emotional desires and drives. Christians are not called to live tepid lives, but are called to the deep joy of emotional balance that comes with spiritual maturity. God gave emotional sensitivity as a gift that serves a positive purpose in life. That purpose is to monitor human happiness.

Emotions are like flashlights in the dark. They keep us from tripping over things we would otherwise not see. But the purpose of a flashlight is not to determine the ultimate direction we are to go, but only to illuminate the immediate path we have chosen. A flashlight can show us the obstacles in the path, but it cannot determine what direction we should go. Similarly, our emotions are not to determine our goals and purposes in life, but only to provide necessary illumination on the path that we travel in order to help keep us from stumbling in the dark.

GOD PROVIDES DIRECTION, NOT HUMAN EMOTIONS

It is God who provides His people with direction and purpose. So, when we allow our emotions to lead, we interfere with God's direction because emotions are always self-centered and self-directed. When feelings or emotions lead, they say, "If it feels good, do it." But when God leads He says, "Do what I command." As you have probably discovered, God doesn't always tell us to do things that feel good. The trials and temptations that God uses to produce spiritual maturity are a case in point.

Psalm 119:67 says, "Before I was afflicted I went astray, But now I keep Your word." Without the affliction and testing of our faith, people naturally drift away from God. People are naturally lazy and selfish. So,

God prods His people to conform to His will, sometimes through the suffering of chastisement, sometimes through the joy of Christ.

Obedience doesn't come naturally. The writer of Hebrews said, "For whom the Lord loves He chastens, And scourges every son whom He receives" (Hebrews 12:6). Just as we must submit to trials and chastening and call on the joy of the Lord for emotional balance, we must also correct an over abundance of emotional joy by calling on the patience of the Lord.

MAY THE LORD SEND YOU TRIALS

A young mother approached a church elder after the service because she had a prayer request. Mothering is not an easy task, children try the patience of their parents.

"I would like you to pray for me that I might learn patience," she asked.

The elder beckoned her to step aside from the flow of traffic. As she did he said to her, "Yes, I will pray every day that the Lord send you tribulation."

She nearly dropped the infant in her arms on top of the toddler at her feet. "No, no!" She said, "I asked for patience!"

The elder opened his Bible to Romans 5:3 and read, "we also glory in tribulations, knowing that tribulation produces perseverance."

Yet, patience is not the final goal either. Patience is simply required in order to reach the final goal. Patience in turn produces spiritual maturity. Maturity is the fruit of patience. Conversely, impatience is a sure sign of immaturity. How many of us have cried, "Lord, give me patience, and give it to me *now!*"

Maturity is marked by a concern for the long run. Maturity does not get distracted by temporary accomplishments or temporary setbacks. In spite of the joys and sorrows of this life, the spiritually mature Christian will hold steady to God's purpose through thick and thin. The voice of maturity is the voice of balance and moderation. Because maturity has experienced the joys and sorrows of life, because maturity has persevered through hell and highwater, maturity is able to hold the passions and disappointments of life in balance, in creative tension, not succumbing to either, but patiently enduring both.

Maturity says, "Though I speak with the tongues of men and of angels, but have not love, I have become sounding brass or a clanging cymbal." Maturity says, "though I have the gift of prophecy, and understand all mysteries and all knowledge, and though I have all faith, so that I could remove mountains, but have not love, I am nothing." Maturity says, "though I bestow all my goods to feed the poor, and though I give my body to be burned, but have not love, it profits me nothing. (Maturity) suffers long and is kind; (Maturity) does not envy; (Maturity) does not parade itself, is not puffed up; does not behave rudely, does not seek its own, is not provoked, thinks no evil; does not rejoice in iniquity, but rejoices in the truth; (Maturity) bears all things, believes all things, hopes all things, endures all things" (1 Corinthians 13:1-7).

And yet, maturity is not the final goal either. It is a means. The end or purpose of God's salvation is not reached without maturity, but maturity itself is not the goal. James said, "But let patience have its perfect work, that you may be perfect and complete, lacking nothing" (James 1:4). Perfection is the goal—perfection in Christ in eternity. Perfection is not possible this side of heaven, of course, but it is the ultimate goal that must drive the Christian's every decision and action.

Too many people hear the word *perfection* and immediately give up on it because they think perfection is impossible in this world. And it is impossible without Christ! It is impossible this side of eternity. But in Christ it is not only possible, it is assured. It is a certainty. In Christ perfection is more certain than the rising of the sun. Like the sun, it is distant, impossible to reach in this earthly flesh. But like the sun, perfection in Christ is not so distant that Christians cannot daily enjoy the benefits of its heat and light.

Do you enjoy that heat? Are you assured of salvation in Christ? Or have you gotten side-tracked by the joys and sorrows of this life?

Lift your eyes to Christ. Lift your hearts and your minds to the Word of the Lord. Lift your spirits to the joy of obedience to Christ, the Lord of God's grace and mercy!

ASK GOD

If any of you lacks wisdom, let him ask of God, who gives to all liberally and without reproach, and it will be given to him. But let him ask in faith, with no doubting, for he who doubts is like a wave of the sea driven and tossed by the wind. For let not that man suppose that he will receive anything from the Lord; he is a double-minded man, unstable in all his ways. —James 1:5-8

Geologists had known for decades that there were great oil reserves in West Texas. But it took time for people to begin to understand what that might mean. In the early days before oil was discovered, ranchers lived in modest West Texas homes tending West Texas flocks and herds that grazed on vast West Texas ranches in the semi-desert West Texas plain. Not unexpectedly, they lived on the surface of the land. The oil was always there, deep in the ground, but there was no knowledge of it nor access to it. So, it did them no good.

Eventually wells were sunk, the oil spewed forth, and the rest is history. The resulting wealth transformed the lives of those who had previously lived in moderation. The oil had been there all the time, but access to it required more than knowledge and the title deed to the property.

Owning a Bible is like owning oil rich property in West Texas (or wherever). It's worth a lot. You might even know about God and Jesus and the biblical plan of salvation. But if you don't dig into it, it is worth very little. Its value must be accessed. We must dig for its wealth.

The believer who is justified through the atoning work of Jesus Christ has a title deed to the grace of God. God's blessings are like the wealth of vast oil deposits. Jesus provides access to the riches of God, who is the source of grace and blessing. God is ready to give all that His children ask in Christ's name. But we must inquire.

GOD GIVES WISDOM

James wrote, "If any of you lacks wisdom...." Who doesn't lack wisdom? James was talking to every Christian, and to each of us. In essence he said, "If you lack wisdom, ask God and He will give it liberally and without reproach." It sounds so easy. But if it's so easy, why aren't more people spiritually wise?

Because asking God for wisdom is like asking a woman for her hand in marriage. Theoretically, it is a simple thing to do, but in reality there are many things that must be taken care of before the question can be broached. You have to believe that this particular woman is the right woman for you. You must be convinced of your own love for her. You must have sufficient reason to believe that the love and relationship are reciprocal. The list goes on. Even after all the questions have been answered, the courage to broach the question turns out to be formidable. The internal debate rages. Am I really doing the right thing? The heart pounds, and awkwardness is overwhelming.

So it is with the Lord. We must believe that God is real, and that God answers prayer, and that God will answer *my* prayer. Before we can ask God anything we must have a relationship with Him. That relationship then needs to become familiar. We need to spend time together in that relationship, trying its trust and proving its faithfulness.

Just as a man cannot expect anything from proposing to a stranger, strangers cannot barge in on God demanding answers or blessings without first establishing some familiarity. We can do that—become familiar with God—because Jesus opened up access to God for all of His people. But we must make use of that access. Jesus opened the door, but we have to go through it.

God gives wisdom "liberally and without reproach." He gives it "generously to all without finding fault" (NIV). In other words, God is not going to blame us or think us stupid because we ask for wisdom. The reason that James includes this phrase is that he knows that people feel self-conscious about asking God for wisdom. Why? Because in the asking we have to admit to ourselves and to God that we don't have it, and that we can't get it on our own. If we could, we would because we long to be self-sufficient like God! And so a certain level of humility must be present. To ask for wisdom, we must admit our own personal lack of wisdom. Again, it sounds easy, but it's not.

EVERYONE IS AN EXPERT

Have you ever noticed that everyone thinks he is an expert in religious matters? It's amazing! You can't tell anyone anything about the Bible. It seems that everyone already knows all they need to know about God, or about the Bible, or about Christ, or about Christianity. People listen to their preachers today, but they have preselected a preacher who already agrees with them. All of our churches and denominations are filled with people who agree with each other. But woe betide if someone ever tells someone else something they don't believe! Everyone has an opinion, and no one is ever wrong in their own eyes. This is the attitude that does not, will not, and cannot seek wisdom.[1]

The difficulty with contemporary evangelism is that people think they know enough to reject the gospel. You can't tell anybody anything. They won't hear it.

"I already know all about that," they say, "but I don't believe it."

It's a funny thing because people don't read the Bible much or study religion much. Yet, they think they already know everything they need to know.

I'm not just talking about people on the street. The same thing is true in the church! Christians of whatever stripe generally think they already know enough to reject Christians of some other stripe. Christians spend precious little time studying the Bible, theology, or doctrine, yet everyone seems to be an expert.

People say, "I know what I believe, and that's enough."

With all this expertise it's no wonder that people don't ask God for wisdom. They don't need to. They're experts already!

The point is that humility is required to ask God for wisdom. Experts are seldom humble. But humility is required before God.

HUMILITY IS REQUIRED

Once people have attained sufficient humility and asked God for His advice, they too often think that He only bestows wisdom miracu-

---

1   If you are unfamiliar with Jeremiah 9, this would be a good time to see that this idea gets a lot of biblical press because it is a common problem.

lously, supernaturally—without study or effort. Can people just go to God in prayer and get wisdom by direct revelation? Well, certainly with God anything is possible (Luke 1:37). But miraculous revelation isn't God's ordinary means of bestowing wisdom. It never has been.

God ordinarily speaks through Scripture, and bestows wisdom through prayer and study of the Scriptures. Wisdom, like salvation, is a gift of God's grace. But God's grace normally works through ordinary means—worship, study of the Scriptures, and prayer. God is able to bestow wisdom and salvation miraculously, but seldom does it happen that way because He has instituted ordinary means through which to accomplish His will. He has done it that way for our sake, not for His. It would be much easier for Him to just zap us. But He doesn't. He calls us to worship, prayer, study, fellowship, and service because it works out better for us in the long run. Consequently, asking God for wisdom also involves a personal commitment to these things.

James also counsels the faithful to "ask in faith, with no doubting" (v. 6). Yet, humility requires self-doubt. Is this a contradiction? Not at all. Faith forbids us to doubt God, so we must conclude that James' caution applies to the doubting of God. Fools do not doubt themselves, and wisdom does not doubt God. When we turn to the Scriptures for wisdom we must not doubt them, but trust them. We must read them, not with the intent of proving them wrong, but with the assurance that they will prove God right.

God is the ground and foundation of all faithfulness. We can be faithful only because God is faithful. His faithfulness provides our faithfulness. We are not to rely upon our own faithfulness, but upon God's faithfulness. Ours is "the faithful God who keeps covenant and mercy for a thousand generations with those who love Him and keep His commandments" (Deuteronomy 7:9).

God's faithfulness provides the kind of stability that will keep us from being "like a wave of the sea driven and tossed by the wind" (v. 6). We can doubt ourselves, our own ability to remain faithful, our own ability to fully understand God's Word—and we must doubt our own strength and ability in order to be humble. But we must not doubt the truth of God's Word, nor the steadfast faithfulness of God's commitment to bring His people to ultimate salvation.

DOUBLE-MINDEDNESS

James also makes mention of the instability of "a double-minded man" (v. 8). In the Old Testament, Elijah accused Israel of being double-minded when he asked, "How long will you falter between two opinions? If the Lord is God, follow Him; but if Baal, follow him"(1 Kings 18:21). Jesus suggested double-mindedness when he said,

> "No one can serve two masters; for either he will hate the one
> and love the other, or else he will be loyal to the one and despise
> the other. You cannot serve God and mammon" (Matthew 6:24).

The double-minded man that James refers to here is a person of divided loyalties and opinions. James raises a very important concern in the church today. The divided loyalty that contemporary Christians wrestle with is the effort to be committed to Christ without giving up any commitment to the world. Who doesn't feel the tension generated by Christ, who pulls in one direction, and the world, which pulls in the other? In this regard most contemporary church members are actually double-minded. Ours is an age of worldly Christianity.

I often say that various aspects of the gospel must be held together in creative tension, suggesting that biblical truth is sometimes many-faceted. But I am not saying that the gospel and the world should be held in tension. We are not to hold Christ and Satan in the same yoke. We are not to blend the values of Scripture with the values of materialism. Nor are we to live Christian lives at church and in our private lives, and succumb to the world at work and in public.

Rather, we are to hold various aspects of the gospel in tension. But doing so is not the double-mindedness that James speaks of, because we are not holding onto two different things. Rather, in the unity of Christ we are holding different aspects of the gospel. We are to believe the whole gospel, not just part of it. We are not free to pick and choose only the parts of God's Word that we agree with or that we understand. We are to believe all of it—even the parts that sometimes seem to contradict each other. We are to hold all of it together in unity, trusting in the faithfulness of God.

Faith and obedience are two aspects of the gospel that must be held in creative tension. True faith does not look at the obstacles that Satan puts in the way. True faith looks only to God. That does not mean that believers ignore or deny the reality of Satan and his minions. Satan is very real, and must be dealt with. Nonetheless believers must keep their eyes on the cross, which means that believers must give God priority in all things.

TRUST IS NOT BLIND

There is a story of an old woman who was known for her obedience to the Lord. Her love and obedience made her shine like a precious jewel. Half jesting, someone once said to her, "I believe that if you thought that the Lord told you to jump through a brick wall, you'd jump."

"If the Lord told me to jump through a wall," she replied, "it would be my business to jump, and it would be God's business to make the hole."

We supply the obedience, God supplies the means and the result.

The relationship between obedience and faith cannot be more clear. This woman knew the essence of trust and true faith. Although we seldom understand every step of the way that we are to walk, although we seldom see the fruit of our faithfulness, we must be "fully convinced that what (God) had promised He is also able to perform" (Romans 4:21). The results are in the hands of the Lord. God is faithful and will complete what He has begun. The writer of Hebrews said it this way, "Let us hold fast the confession of our hope without wavering, for He who promised is faithful" (10:23).

Let's ask God for wisdom. Let's trust God's Word to provide that wisdom. Let's not pick and choose which parts of the Bible to believe and obey, but let's hold to it all. Let's worship, and study the Scriptures, and pray, trusting in God's faithfulness. Let's be obedient, and trust God to provide the results.

This is easy to say, but it cannot be done apart from the Lord. Ours is not a works-righteous faith, but a works-abundant faith.

FADING PURSUITS

Let the lowly brother glory in his exaltation, but the rich in his humiliation, because as a flower of the field he will pass away. For no sooner has the sun risen with a burning heat than it withers the grass; its flower falls, and its beautiful appearance perishes. So the rich man also will fade away in his pursuits.   *—James 1:9-11*

James now provides a practical example regarding his admonition in verse 2, "count it all joy when you fall into various trials." The example he brings forward is the trial of money. Monetary concerns cause many otherwise faithful people to lose their way. Jesus said that "the cares of this world and the deceitfulness of riches choke the word" (Matthew 13:22), causing unfruitfulness. Because we live in the wealthiest period of human history, we must take special care in this regard.

Most people think that the trials of wealth are related to poverty, and indeed poverty brings many trials and difficulties to the faithful and unfaithful alike. But equally troublesome, and far more subtle, are the difficulties that accompany wealth. My dad was fond of saying that those who have a lot of money have a lot of headaches to go with it. He preferred not to have the headaches.

Jesus taught that money is not an end in itself—not a goal or purpose in life, but a means to a greater end. He also said that people "cannot serve God and mammon" (Matthew 6:24). It's not that they can't try! It's just not possible. One always takes precedence over the other. The love of money distracts us from our responsibility to serve God. And what is worse, people find themselves rationalizing their commitment to mammon in the name of God!

"God wants me to be rich."

"I can serve more effectively because I have more."

But neither of the above rationalizations are true.

There are two classes of people who think too much about money —the rich and the poor. Because the rich overvalue it, they spend too much time glorying in their ability to get it, and plotting ways to keep it. And because the poor also overvalue it, they spend too much time lamenting their lack of it, and plotting ways to strike it rich by stealth, gambling, or vainly hoping for good fortune. The rich and the poor actually have much in common because of their overly zealous concerns about money.

The worship of mammon by rich and poor alike is evidenced by their incessant financial concern. Consequently, James suggests that an overactive concern for worldly wealth imposes a trial or test upon personal faithfulness. When acquiring money becomes a purpose in life, it detracts from the time and energy that we have for God's greater purpose. Everyone needs money to live, of course, but money is a by-product. It is not a thing-in-itself. It is a measure, a means, and nothing more. While it is valuable, it does not and cannot constitute a value upon which to live.

James said, "Let the lowly brother glory in his exaltation, but the rich in his humiliation" (v. 9). In other words, let the poor be inspired by the glory of salvation, and let the wealthy be admonished by the mercy of salvation. The poor need to be uplifted by salvation, while the rich need to be humbled by it. Salvation knows neither wealth nor poverty. Money has nothing to do with salvation. A different measure, another value functions at the judgment seat of Christ. In Christ, at judgment, the presence or absence of worldly wealth is immaterial. Such distinctions are of no concern to the Lord of salvation.

But Christians know that! This is not new information for believers. However, it is so easy for people to hear the Bible's teaching about money and wealth, to hear that it makes no difference for salvation, and to turn the plain teaching of Scripture around and use it to justify personal selfishness.

JUSTIFYING SELFISHNESS

The wealthy justify themselves by thinking that, because money doesn't matter to God, it won't keep them from salvation. They try to convince themselves that their wealth and worldly pursuits have no effect upon their salvation. So, they conclude, they are free to do with their wealth whatever they want.

But their conclusion is in error because Christianity is not a matter of doing what *we* want, but doing what *God* wants. While wealth does not play any role in salvation, it does play a role in damnation.

The wealthy need to consider the parable of the rich, young ruler. Here was a man who was faithful in so many ways. His faithful religious practice, no doubt, would put us all to shame. His one fault was that his money was more important to him that the Lord. And when Jesus told him so, "He went away sorrowful" (Matthew 19:23) because he could not value Christ more than he valued his money.

THE PRIDE OF POVERTY

At this point the poor begin to sit up straight because they know that *their* money will never get between them and the Lord—but only because they don't have any! If they did, they would more than likely follow the rich young ruler in a flash. It almost seems nonsensical to say that the wealth of the poor doesn't stand in the way of their faithfulness. It doesn't stand in the way—not because they have conquered its temptations, but because it's a non-issue. Many of the poor need to hear Paul's admonition to Timothy that "the love of money" (1 Timothy 6:10) is the tenacious root of evil. It is not money that gets in the way of salvation, but the *love* of money displaces the necessary love of the Lord. Wealth and plenty are not the problem! Heaven itself is a place of great wealth.

Yet, many who are poor fare no better than the rich in this regard because the poor are as often blinded by financial concerns as the rich. They have a different point of view, but are just as much consumed with financial concern. James' point is that all who are in Christ are equal with regard to salvation. Ideally, the poor who need encouragement can glory in salvation, and the rich who need humbling can thank God for His mercy. But human experience is often very different.

The inequalities of disposable income interfere with many Christian relationships. The jealousies and frustrations of not being able to keep up with the proverbial Joneses keep many poorer Christians from fellowshipping in the suburbs. And similar concerns keep many suburban Christians away from small inner-city churches.

We all struggle to make ends meet. At whatever monetary level we live, there never seems to be enough money! But because we struggle at different levels, the inequalities often sour Christian fellowship. The well-to-do are embarrassed to be seen with the poor, and the poor drool all over the rich. However, James is calling Christians beyond such petty concerns. James encourages us to forget the inequalities of the world, and focus on the glory of salvation. James calls us to get our eyes off the world and onto the cross. James calls Christians beyond financial concerns altogether.

CHRISTIANS STARVING THEIR OWN CHURCHES

Could it be that Christians are financially starving their churches? Most churches suffer the symptoms of corporate anorexia. They are starving in the midst of plenty. Too many Christians are constrained by old habits of giving and tithing. Has your church giving kept pace with inflation? Has it kept pace with your salary? Has it kept pace with your financial portfolio? Do you give freely? Or do you use your weekly giving as a political weapon to encourage things you like and discourage things you don't like? Do you give freely, or try to buy control and influence? Is your church worthy of your support?

Such thoughts should not be surprising or foreign to Christians because such things happen in the real world all the time. Don't they? But is this approach to stewardship scriptural? Is it God's way? If Christians handled their money God's way (by tithing and providing direct financial services) churches would be awash in money! Budgets would increase ten-fold or more.

However, it would be a travesty to suggest that money alone could solve the problems found in most churches. Money alone won't solve our problems because our real problem lies much deeper. Our real problem is about obedience to the Lord in everything. We have a heart problem, a faith problem.

Don't get me wrong. Ours is not a completely faithless generation, not by any stretch of the imagination. But neither are we as faithful as we could be.

The symptoms are classic. Churches struggle with budgets. They worry excessively about statistics—finances and worship attendance, but care too little about genuine Christian growth. Churches today are self-concerned and ingrown, both those that are growing and those that are not. Too often, financial giving is politically motivated, rather than being a simple expression of faithfulness.

This criticism is not about the size of the gift. Large gifts are not more generous than small. In fact, usually the opposite is true. Large gifts usually come with strings attached because the givers want to make the most of their gift. They want a good return on their investment. They want to get something, usually their own way.

NUMBERING OR MEASURING GOD'S PEOPLE

Church growth experts study the measurable characteristics of growing churches and suggest many helpful things. But the real elements for success in the Lord are immeasurable—commitment, faithfulness, and obedience. Our responsibility is faithfulness to God's Word. Growth—the result, the fruit—is God's concern. The lesson that is yet to be learned in our time is that imitating the characteristics of a growing church will not produce faithfulness.

The same thing is true about individuals. The imitation of Christian characteristics will not produce faithful Christians. Such imitation is merely works-righteousness. When people do the things that Christians do because they want the blessings that other Christians have, they are paddling down the stream of works-righteousness, trying to manipulate God's grace. And what is worse, they do it because they covet what others have.

We understand that as individuals. We are quite clear about works-righteousness regarding individual spirituality. But when we apply the sociological insights of church growth studies upon the church—trying to cause it to grow, we are guilty of corporate works-righteousness, as if doing certain things will cause God to grant His blessing. The application of market strategies to the church is a kind of corporate works-righteousness. It may work in the sense of bringing church growth, but it cannot produce faithful Christians. In fact, over time it will mitigate against faithfulness because it is not built upon faithfulness.

We need to quit worrying about church growth for a while and start worrying about personal faithfulness. We need to worry about salvation, and about teaching the Bible to our children and grandchildren. We need to worry about our marriages and our families. We need to worry about prayer and tithing—the things of the heart. Christians today are too concerned with trying to do God's job, more concerned about results and growth than they are about their own Christian responsibility to be faithful. The priorities of contemporary churches are not operating according to God's priorities.

Consequently, Christians need to turn to Christ. *Christians* need to turn to Christ because, as they concern themselves with the Sunday morning schedules, or what color the carpet should be, they concern themselves with their own selfish desires and take their eyes off the cross. As we find ourselves thinking about coffee and cookies after worship, we are not thinking about God's Word. Contemporary Christians have become Marthas rather than Marys.

Can the church repent? Can Christians begin again in the Lord? Can you do that? Are *you* willing to repent? Or don't you need to?

At risk are not only the life and mission of your particular church, but the individual destinies of God's people. To repent means "to think again," to rethink what we are doing and how we are doing it. It means to go in another direction, to turn around.

Church renewal or revival, like spiritual growth, begins with personal repentance.

DRAWN AWAY

Blessed is the man who endures temptation; for when he has been approved, he will receive the crown of life which the Lord has promised to those who love Him. Let no one say when he is tempted, "I am tempted by God"; for God cannot be tempted by evil, nor does He Himself tempt anyone. But each one is tempted when he is drawn away by his own desires and enticed. Then, when desire has conceived, it gives birth to sin; and sin, when it is full-grown, brings forth death. —James 1:12-15

A man was filling out a job application. The secretary gave him a form and told him to answer all the questions. As usual the form had a series of questions about his health and history. One of the questions asked if he had ever been arrested.

"No," he answered.

Beside it was another question with space for an extended answer. The other question asked "Why?"

Following the secretary's instructions he wrote, "Never got caught."

Verse 12 reads, "Blessed is the man who endures temptation." The man filling out the job application had not endured temptation. He had succumbed to it. The fact that he had not been caught had no effect upon his guilt. If he was a Christian he also misunderstood God's instructions regarding sin and temptation. Like many contemporary Christians, he believed that the worst thing about sin was not doing wrong, but getting caught.

James teaches the exact opposite. Wrong is wrong, whether you get caught or not. Besides, God will catch all sinners at the final judgment, when He judges hearts and motives. There will be no escaping God's judgment. He will expose every sin.

SIN GROWS ON PEOPLE

People do not begin life as hardened criminals. Rather, criminals are grown bit by bit. They are drawn into sin and crime a little at a time, as they are drawn away from God's love and away from God's law. It happens slowly over time.

In contrast, God promises a crown of life to believers who persevere in faithfulness. The crown of life is an allusion to a race, a competition. Unlike speed races where there are few winners, the race James refers to is an endurance race. It is also different from most competitions because all who finish are winners.

The promises of God are given "to those who love Him" (v. 12). Loving God is exactly where the spiritual rubber meets the material road. The final crown is given, not simply to those who suffer—for all suffer in this sinful world, but to those who love the Lord. Love of the Lord triumphs over suffering and temptation.

James affirms that the most important issue in life is loving God. The love of God will keep Christians from falling for the temptations of Satan. And precisely because of this fact, Satan's most effective measures are intended to keep people from loving God. If Satan can wreck the relationship between you and the Lord, he doesn't need to worry about the fruit of that relationship. So Satan makes every effort to tempt people to sin, to draw them away from God by whatever means possible—and Satan's means are many and most effective.

The thing to notice is that Satan is the tempter, not God. Satan suckers people into his web of sin by tempting them with the good things they normally desire. The Lord does not tempt people. But God will certainly chasten His people. "What son is there whom a father does not chasten?" (Hebrews 12:7).

GOD MADE ME THE WAY I AM

Today, we hear many people argue that "God has made me the way I am," implying that whatever sin they are involved in is okay because it originates in God. Such a defense usually applies to the sins of lust and gluttony. The argument is that because God created the body, whatever the body desires must be okay with God, otherwise He would not have made it the way He did. We rationalize that our lust or glut-tony is not a sin. It is simply a normal aspect of being human.

In essence, those who employ this argument blame their sinful behavior on God. "God made me the way I am," they argue, "therefore, what I am is God's fault." They blame God for making them sinners, implying that God causes sin. But God didn't make sinners. God made humanity, yes, and He made them male and female, and He made them very good. Man's fall came through Adam, and Adam's fall came by Satan, not God.

The contemporary argument sounds just like Adam in the garden, "The woman whom You gave to be with me, she gave me of the tree, and I ate" (Genesis 3:12). It wasn't Adam's fault, Eve gave it to him! It was her fault—"the woman *You* gave...me." Ultimately of course, he blamed God because God had given him the woman. It's a dodge that just doesn't hold water.

Eve fared no better. She blamed the serpent. "The serpent deceived me, and I ate" (Genesis 3:13). The comedian Flip Wilson used to say, "The devil made me do it." Contemporary society has completely bought into Flip Wilson's joke about demonic possession. Now we can argue that if it is not God's fault, then it must be Satan's fault. People today don't take responsibility for anything. We have become a society of self-confessed and self-absorbed victims. The culprits of sin and crime are never the people who actually commit the offensive acts.

We understand drunkards and gluttons to be chemically imbal-anced. They aren't sinners, their blood is chemically flawed. Is it God's fault for making them that way? Are criminals simply victims of poor parenting or inadequate socialization—or both? Are they merely victims of psychological abuse or social deprivation? And since God brought them into their particular family or situation, is it again His fault? Are adulterers victims of mental and emotional cruelty by a spouse, or over-active glands? Most refuse to see themselves as responsible for their behavior. After all, God brought them into the wrong relationship. God gave them their glands. He knew their weaknesses. Again it is easy to blame God.

All of these excuses have a bit of truth in them, but their primary purpose is to blame someone or something else for *my* behavior. In contrast, Scripture says that everyone is a sinner, and that people are responsible for their own sin.

FREEDOM AND RESPONSIBILITY

It's curious how Americans pride themselves on their freedom. Personal freedom is celebrated as the cornerstone of American character. But did you ever notice how Americans fail to claim personal responsibility for sin? The truth is that if people are not responsible for their own behavior, they cannot be free. Freedom and responsibility go together. You can't have one without the other. If we are free, we must be responsible, but if we are not responsible, then we cannot be free. But we cannot have it both ways. We cannot be both free and irresponsible. We can be free and responsible, or we can be irresponsible but not free. Which is it?

Contemporary Christians even use Scripture to defend sin. The creation story of Genesis 1 is a favorite. The argument is that everything God created was good. Therefore, whatever the body craves is okay because everything was created good. The argument is fine as far as it goes. The problem is that it doesn't go to Genesis 3. It ignores sin and the Fall. The reality of sin is denied by such an argument, but it is not denied by Scripture.

The Fall of man brought sin into the world when Adam acted contrary to God's command. Sin is not good, nor are the cravings of sinful men. Sin thrives on temptation. And temptation is Satan's most effective weapon. But, James tells us, "God cannot be tempted by evil, nor does He Himself tempt anyone" (v. 13). So, wherever temptation arises it is Satan's work.

Temptation differs from chastening and inspiration. Temptation is a lure, an enticement. Fishermen know that a lure is a fake. A lure is not what it appears to be. Its whole purpose is to deceive. It looks like food to a fish, but isn't. An effective lure is very good at making a fish believe that it is something that it isn't. The purpose of the lure is to attract by pretense. It pretends to be a little fish or a bug, shimmering and glimmering in the water. But it is not a fish or a bug, it is death in drag, masquerading as something it is not.

Temptation is not God's method. God does not pretend. God does not entice. God does not lure people into salvation like a snake oil salesman selling his wares to the unwary. Rather, like the Father that He is,

God commands. His command itself is inspiration and is intended to motivate His people to obedience. But when God's commands are not heeded, He brings chastisement upon His people in order to bring them back to obedience. Both inspiration and chastisement, unlike temptation, are exactly what they seem to be. One is a self-motivator, the other is a kind of goad to improve behavior. They don't pretend to be anything else. God provides blessings for obedience and cursings for disobedience (Deuteronomy 28). God has always operated that way, and still does.

There are indeed consequences to all human actions and behaviors. God's method is to teach the truth about wrong behavior by allowing His people to suffer the consequences of their behavior—not because He likes punishment, but because He wants us to understand that the world He created good has good rules, which He also created. And living by those good rules brings about the fulfillment of the good that God created. Living in God's world requires living by God's rules because it is His world. He made it. So, God chastises His children because He loves them, and He wants them to prosper according to His grace and mercy.

God doesn't deceive His people. He can't lie. He can't pretend to be something He isn't. God doesn't lure people into heaven. He commands His people to obey Him of their own free will. His descriptions of heaven and of salvation are true, and can be trusted. So are His invitations and commands. God does not pretend. He speaks the truth. He can do no other.

However, God does inspire people to greater faithfulness by encouraging and helping them to grow in personal faithfulness. Inspiration, unlike Satan's seduction, does not deceive. God inspires people by always telling the truth and demonstrating his trustworthiness. Unlike Satan's lure, God's truth is always exactly what it appears to be. Its eternal attractiveness is aimed at the soul, not at the temporary pleasures of the body. Everything that God promises about salvation is absolutely true.

James agrees with Paul when he says that desire produces sin, and sin produces death. "For the wages of sin is death," said Paul, "but the gift of God is eternal life in Christ Jesus our Lord" (Romans 6:23). We stand convicted, not just by our tendency to avoid personal responsibility for our sins, but by our love of sin. We are sinners one and all, and must stand as sinners at the bar of God's judgment. God will not countenance our denial of personal responsibility.

How will you plead? Will you tell God that you are not guilty? Will you deny your guilt? Or will you throw yourself on the mercy of the court? God will surely grant mercy, but only in or through Christ. Those who are in Christ can appeal to God's mercy because Christ has paid the penalty for their sin. Christ died so that His people might live.

Jesus said, "Come to Me, all you who labor and are heavy laden, and I will give you rest" (Matthew 11:28). Jesus said, "If anyone desires to come after Me, let him deny himself, and take up his cross, and follow Me" (Matthew 16:24). Jesus said, "Let the little children come to Me" (Matthew 19:14). Jesus said, "All that the Father gives Me will come to Me, and the one who comes to Me I will by no means cast out" (John 6:37). Jesus said, "No one can come to Me unless the Father who sent Me draws him" (John 6:44).

God is calling. God is drawing His people to Himself. God demands that every sinner come to judgment! You will come, that much is not in question. But will you come in Christ? Or without Him?

No Shadow of Turning

Do not be deceived, my beloved brethren. Every good gift and every
perfect gift is from above, and comes down from the Father of lights,
with whom there is no variation or shadow of turning. Of His own
will He brought us forth by the word of truth, that we might be a
kind of firstfruits of His creatures. So then, my beloved brethren, let
every man be swift to hear, slow to speak, slow to wrath; for the
wrath of man does not produce the righteousness of God.

—James 1:16-20

A Christian grocer was in financial difficulty because his customers charged up their bills more readily than they paid them. Many of them belonged to the same church and believed it to be sinful for a fellow Christian to begrudge the fact that they were too poor to pay the bill. Neither could the grocer take them to court. Brothers in Christ were supposed to avoid secular courts. Again and again they told the grocer that they didn't have the money to pay their bill.

He wondered what the faithful response should be. Should he simply believe them, when every evidence suggested that they were not telling the whole truth? They lived in nice homes, wore nice clothes, drove good cars. Should he go bankrupt because of their delinquency? And what about his Christian obligation to them? He prayed and searched the Bible for advice.

Finally an idea came to him. He posted the following bulletin on the front door: "On this bulletin board, thirty days from now, will appear the names of all those who have been indebted to me for one year or more and who, after repeated requests, have refused to pay. Some have told me that they are unable to pay, but they are able to have beautiful homes, drive nice cars, and have other things that only money can buy."

Results followed immediately. Accounts were paid. And the grocer's action was consistent with Christian love and responsibility. He refused to believe the delusions of others, and by doing so he refused to allow them to continue in deceit and dishonesty. Love believes all things that encourage honesty and virtue in others. Love does not believe lies, but endeavors to correct them because falsehood and deceit are injurious to the object and purpose of love.

James wrote, "Do not be deceived" (v. 16), which means that it is quite possible for Christians to be deceived. Christians can be quite wrong about many things, and still be saved. Christians are not saved because they believe correctly, but by God's grace alone. Right belief itself does not save. Rather, salvation engages right belief through right behavior—not perfectly, nor all at once. But little by little Christians grow in godliness and right understanding. James' words addressed the misunderstanding that God was the author of temptation. "No," said James, "God tempts no one." He couldn't say it more clearly.

Falsehood is contrary to God's nature. Not only will God not deceive His people, but as James goes on to say, "every good and perfect gift is from (God)" (v. 17). God is not only good, and gives good and perfect gifts, but God is unchanging. God's character is immutable and incorruptible. As Paul said, "Jesus Christ is the same yesterday, today, and forever" (Hebrews 13:8). So, all good gifts come from God. God's motives and intentions are always honest and honorable, and they will never change. It is impossible for God, who is light, to be obscured by any degree of shadow. His light, like His goodness, is pure.

CHRISTIANS CAN BE WRONG

God's truth shines forth clearly. God will never obscure or change that truth. Yet, it is possible for Christians to be wrong about God, to misunderstand and misrepresent Him. God Himself will never present His truth inaccurately or insufficiently, yet we can still get it wrong because Satan specializes in spiritual error and deceit, and Satan is a mighty foe. Satan is not as powerful as God, but he is much more powerful than we are. This is only to say that all error and insufficiency must be attributed either to ourselves or Satan, but never to God. Any attempt to do so only reveals a misunderstanding of the character and nature of God.

The application of this truth is twofold. First, it should throw us into deep study of God's Word with the assurance that what we find there will be trustworthy. If you are not drawn more deeply into God's Word by James' insight, then you haven't really heard or understood it. The understanding that Scripture and Scripture alone is the only trustworthy expositor of God's will in this fallen world of relativity and falsehood necessitates serious study and reliance upon it. If it seems that the value of Bible study is too often extolled by believers, it is only because you have not yet applied this discipline of joy and victory in your own life. Those who study the Bible the most best realize the insufficiency of their own efforts. Those who just skim the surface of Scripture are often the first to acclaim their superior knowledge. The old adage applies: you can lead a horse to water, but he must drink of his own desire.

The second application carries into the following verses in James' letter. Here we find a caution regarding the human tendency of error and false belief. It is much easier to believe what isn't true, than to submit to the demands of God's truth. It is not that God's truth is hard to understand, but that it runs counter to our natural tendencies and desires. People don't want to believe God's Word because it quashes their self-esteem.

You can observe this natural tendency in children between the ages of five and twenty, who are absolutely convinced that they know everything. By the time they reach adolescence they are just as certain that one's age, rather than contributing to wisdom, actually detracts from it. By fifteen they are appalled at how little their parents and other adults actually know. Most of what teenagers call wisdom runs directly counter to their parents' counsel, and especially to godly authority—Scripture. Why is this?

It can only be attributed to the natural tendency of human beings to believe in themselves. "I'm right and everybody else is wrong," they think. "I'm right, and God and Scripture or history has nothing to offer." Or if they don't actually think the thought, they act as if they believe it.

This second application of James' insight is a corrective to this natural tendency. "Let every man be swift to hear, slow to speak, slow to wrath" (v. 19), says James. Gordon Keddie says that at the heart of verse nineteen

> "is the humble realization of the need to learn and the concomitant awareness that if I'm endlessly spouting my ignorance, I can't be absorbing your wisdom...or the Lord's. ... If you can't listen it's because you're doing the talking, neither can you listen if you aren't paying attention. ...You can't be listening to the right things, if you waste your attention on unprofitable things."[1]

Godly wisdom begins with hearing God's Word. Paul said it this way,

> "How then shall they call on Him in whom they have not believed? And how shall they believe in Him of whom they have not heard? And how shall they hear without a preacher?" (Romans 10:14).

PREACHING ALONE CAN MAKE YOU SICK

Preaching is not a replacement for Bible study. Many people think that coming to church and listening to the preacher is enough to sustain their spiritual health. But preaching was never intended to be the main source of spiritual nourishment. To feed on preaching alone, without devotion to systematic Bible study will quickly lead to spiritual impoverishment.

Personal Bible study and prayer are the main staples. Preaching is a supplement, a vitamin given to ensure that you are getting all the essentials. Vitamin-rich gospel preaching is needed to supplement our contemporary fast-food spiritual diets. But if all you do is take vitamins and never feed on the milk and meat of personal prayer and study you will get spiritually sick. Your life and faith will actually be malnourished. You will have no spiritual strength or vitality. Not even great preaching can replace the need for personal engagement of Scripture.

Godly wisdom begins with listening. We must be willing to listen. But as the children's song advises, "Be careful little ears, what you hear." Just because wisdom requires hearing doesn't mean that everything that can be heard contributes to wisdom. Our hearing must not only be

---

1   *The Practical Christian*, Gordon Keddie, Evangelical Press, England, 1989, p. 67.

engaged, it must also be discerning. As contemporary labels warn, some discretion is advised.

Imagine that you have a friend who is completely trustworthy. You have never known your friend to do anything that would cause doubt or suspicion. Then someone tells you a lie about your friend. Even though you don't believe the lie, hearing it plants a seed of doubt in your mind. You might try to dismiss it because you know it is a lie, but it has already done its work in you. If you then hear another lie about your friend, even the same lie repeated by someone else, that seed of doubt begins to take root. If you hear enough lies about a trusted friend, even though he has done nothing to cause you to distrust him, even though you make every effort to continue to trust him, you may find that your relationship with him begins to deteriorate.

So it is with Christ. Ungodly sinners outnumber God's elect—genuine Christians—by far. Jesus said, "narrow is the gate and difficult is the way which leads to life, and there are few who find it" (Matthew 7:14). When we listen to those who are on the "broad …way that leads to destruction" (Matthew 7:13), we are listening to lies about God. The more we listen, the more we believe ungodly lies. It was Hitler's insight that people will believe a lie if it is only repeated often enough. The ungodly have learned his lesson well. The truth is that we hear such lies all the time on TV, in the press, on the Internet, from our friends—even from pulpits. We accommodate ourselves to such lies only at the expense of our relationship with Christ.

So, while we need to be "swift to hear" we must also be careful about what we listen to. James also says that we should be "slow to speak" and "slow to wrath." These admonitions go together because they are related. In chapter three James will tell us that

> "the tongue is a fire, a world of iniquity. The tongue is so set
> among our members that it defiles the whole body, and sets on
> fire the course of nature; and it is set on fire by hell" (James 3:6).

Again, the old adage applies: it is better to be quiet and have people think you are a fool, than to open your mouth and prove it.

You might wonder why there should be so much caution about hearing and speaking only what is right, and good, and trustworthy. Must we really protect ourselves and our families from so much? Must there be such distrust among people? Can't we trust our friends and neighbors more than that?

The reason for the distrust has less to do with your particular friends and neighbors than with the sinful nature of man. Jesus taught His disciples that it is "not what goes into the mouth defiles a man; but what comes out of the mouth" (Matthew 15:11). He was alluding to the depravity of man. People are by nature sinful and morally corrupt. Some are worse than others, of course. But, in truth, all are so corrupt as to make any differences between them without significance in God's eyes.

James carries this thought further when he says that "the wrath of man does not produce the righteousness of God" (v. 20). Sometimes we think that if we just set our minds to a task, we can do anything. People often think that they could be good if they wanted to, that they could measure up to God's standard of righteousness if they put their minds to it. This is very much the attitude of the contemporary mind.

People don't like to think of themselves as depraved, but that is what Scripture tells us. Paul, writing to Titus said, "To the pure all things are pure, but to those who are defiled and unbelieving nothing is pure; but even their mind and conscience are defiled" (Titus 1:15). The implication seems to be that there might be some people who are pure. But in his letter to the Romans Paul made sure that we understand that Scripture testifies that none are pure.

> "There is none righteous, no, not one; There is none who understands; There is none who seeks after God. They have all turned aside; They have together become unprofitable; There is none who does good, no, not one" (Romans 3:10-12).

When James said that "the wrath of man does not produce the righteousness of God" (v. 20) he was saying that man cannot by his own strength and power make himself righteous. Neither anger nor self-determination can change human nature. "Can the Ethiopian change his skin or the leopard its spots?" (Jeremiah 13:23).

DEVOLUTION, NOT EVOLUTION

Contrary to evolutionary theory, man is not evolving, but devolving. Left to our own devices, people naturally wax worse and worse over time, just as Scripture and history testify. Consequently, it is only by the grace of God that anyone is saved, that anyone is able to stand before the righteous God and plead the blood of Christ. Only because of the atoning sacrifice of Jesus Christ, who died for the sins of His people, in their place, can anyone be saved. There is simply no other way.

> "For the love of Christ compels us, because we judge thus: that if
> One died for all, then all died; and He died for all, that those
> who live should live no longer for themselves, but for Him who
> died for them and rose again" (2 Corinthians 5:14-15).

Christians are called to repentance, not just once in a lifetime, but to a life of repentance. I don't mean that people need to "go forward" or "confess Christ" again and again. Rather, living a life of repentance means always seeking God's direction to correct our faulty ways. It has little to do with going forward at a revival meeting.

People need to think again about their own faithfulness, about their own commitment to Christ because just as soon as someone thinks that he has it, he has actually lost it.

Think again.

Are you really saved? Is your gospel tree bearing fruit? We must remember that "every tree that does not bear good fruit (will be) cut down and thrown into the fire" (Matthew 7:19).

BE DOERS

Therefore lay aside all filthiness and overflow of wickedness, and receive with meekness the implanted word, which is able to save your souls. But be doers of the word, and not hearers only, deceiving yourselves. For if anyone is a hearer of the word and not a doer, he is like a man observing his natural face in a mirror; for he observes himself, goes away, and immediately forgets what kind of man he was. But he who looks into the perfect law of liberty and continues in it, and is not a forgetful hearer but a doer of the word, this one will be blessed in what he does. If anyone among you thinks he is religious, and does not bridle his tongue but deceives his own heart, this one's religion is useless. Pure and undefiled religion before God and the Father is this: to visit orphans and widows in their trouble, and to keep oneself unspotted from the world. —James 1:21-27*

Verse 21 begins with the word *therefore*, which means that the verse concludes what has gone before. "Therefore lay aside... and receive...." Two actions are called for, lay aside what is negative, and receive what is positive. Lay aside filthiness and wickedness, and receive "the implanted word."

Earlier James told us that God "of His own will brought us forth by the word of truth" (v. 18), indicating that God's Word is a means of grace. He said that God's Word is a vehicle of regeneration. While salvation comes by grace alone through faith alone in Christ alone, Christ and His Holy Spirit cannot be separated from God's Word. Consequently, there is no salvation apart from God's Word. Grace and faith are bound up together with Christ in God's Word.

Notice also that James refers to it as "the implanted word," or "engrafted word" in the KJV. The idea is that God's Word is alive, like a seed or branch that sprouts and grows. God's Word "is able," says James, "to save your souls" (v. 21). This is a very important piece of information. God's Word is the object of faith in that it cannot be separated from Christ and His Holy Spirit. They are different, yet bound up together. So, the Word is a means of grace and, therefore, a means of salvation.

Yet, James adds another caution to keep us from misunderstanding him. Yes, God's Word is an effective means of salvation, but the mere hearing of it is impotent apart from the presence of the Holy Spirit. The hearing of God's Word, while necessary, is not sufficient for salvation. While faith comes by hearing, it does not end with hearing. If I give you a command, and you tell me that you hear me, but you fail to do what is commanded, it is the same as if you did not hear me. Hearing God's Word, which must always be interpreted as a command, but without making the appropriate response, is not real or biblical hearing. Hearing means responding to the command.

James means that real hearing requires a response. The consequence of hearing without action is the hypocrisy of self-deception. God does not deceive people, but people can and do deceive themselves. Hearing without obedience is Jesus' definition of hypocrisy. He called the Pharisees "Hypocrites!" and affirmed what Isaiah prophesied about them, saying, "These people draw near to Me with their mouth, And honor Me with their lips, But their heart is far from Me" (Matthew 15:8-9). He meant that the failure of their belief in God manifested in their failure to act upon God's Word.

This idea that works must accompany faith, that behavior is a part of belief, is not unique to James. People sometimes mistakenly think that because salvation is by faith, and not by works, that works are unnecessary. But listen to the testimony of Scripture:

> "Not everyone who says to Me, 'Lord, Lord,' shall enter the kingdom of heaven, but he who does the will of My Father in heaven" (Matthew 7:21).

> "For whoever does the will of My Father in heaven is My brother and sister and mother" (Matthew 12:50).

"But why do you call Me 'Lord, Lord,' and do not do the things
which I say?" (Luke 6:46).

"…blessed are those who hear the word of God and keep it!"
(Luke 11:28).

"If you know these things, blessed are you if you do them" (John
13:17).

Paul said, "for not the hearers of the law are just in the sight of
God, but the doers of the law will be justified" (Romans 2:13). Jesus
said, "If you love Me, keep My commandments" (John 14:15). John
said, "Now by this we know that we know Him, if we keep His
commandments" (1 John 2:3).

This is not a new idea that James thought up, it is everywhere in
Scripture. It means that Christians are not exempt from the Ten Commandments. We are not free to ignore God's Law. Rather, we have
been saved that we may apply ourselves to God's Word and God's Law
without the fear of failure. Christians are to be obedient to God's Law,
not in order to achieve salvation, but in thankfulness for the salvation
provided by the free grace of Jesus Christ.

We know that the ceremonial law changed when Christ, our high
priest, sacrificed Himself for the atonement of our sins. That is a fundamental difference between the Old Testament and the New. By His
sacrificial death, Jesus replaced the Old Testament priesthood, so all of
the ceremonial sacrifices are obsolete in Christ. The faithful no longer
need to bring birds and sheep and bulls for sacrifice.

But the moral and civil law—the heart of which is the Ten Commandments—still stand. For instance, because Christ is our High Priest,
the Sabbath observance has moved from Saturday to Sunday, the day of
His resurrection. The change of Sabbath observance is symbolic of the
change of the priesthood and the ceremonial law. Nonetheless, the
principle of the Sabbath and all the other Commandments remains in
tact, but not as a means of salvation. Rather, our obedience is a loving
and obedient response to the salvation given in Christ.

Similarly, the other Commandments remain in force. Real love of
Christ as Lord and Savior produces obedience to Christ's commands.
Jesus said, "Do not think that I came to destroy the Law or the
Prophets. I did not come to destroy but to fulfill" (Matthew 5:17).

GOD'S LAW IS A MIRROR

James speaks of the law as a mirror. "He who looks into the perfect law of liberty and continues in it…will be blessed in what he does" (v. 25). Notice how he describes it: "the perfect law of liberty." We normally think of law and liberty as being opposed to one another, but James holds them together in creative tension. Perfect liberty requires obedience to God's law. And perfect obedience requires conformity to Scripture, not by coercion, but by genuine willingness.

Christ holds up God's law as a mirror that we may see ourselves as God sees us. I look into a mirror and see that my face is dirty, but I don't use the mirror to wash my face. It would be foolishness to take the mirror down and rub my dirty face with it. The purpose of the mirror is not to clean the face, but to reveal the dirt. The purpose of the mirror is to send the person with a dirty face to the water to wash. The mirror does not clean. It only reveals.

Similarly, anyone who tries to be saved by keeping the Ten Commandments or living by the Sermon on the Mount is like a person who tries to wash with a mirror. It cannot be done. He will only smear the dirt on his face and smudge the mirror in the process. God's Law is like a mirror, it reveals human sin, but it cannot cleanse it. Only Christ can cleanse sin in the waters of regeneration. I don't mean that baptism cleanses the sin, baptism is only a ceremony. Baptism is not a guarantee of regeneration. Christ alone renews the heart by spiritually cleansing sin through the provision of a new heart.

The death of Christ satisfied God's order and His sense of justice. Christ died in the place of believers. His perfection satisfied God's sacrificial requirements, and established God's decree of mercy for those who are in Christ, those who are obedient to His authority.

Who might that be? Scripture clearly says that all who *will* come *may* come to Christ, all who *can* come *ought* to come to Christ for salvation. Whoever comes *will* be—not *might* be—saved *from* God's wrath, and *for* God's love, "…whosoever believes in Him shall not perish but have everlasting life" (John 3:16).

You are reading this, and that is certainly a step in the right direction. You may even attend a church. But coming to church is not the same as coming to Christ. Coming forward is not the same as coming to Christ. Many come to church—and even come forward—who never really come to Christ. To come to Christ means to willingly give yourself to His authority in obedience to His Word.

Are you obedient to the Word of Christ? What about the Ten Commandments? Do you really love Jesus? Can you even recite the Ten Commandments?

BRIDLE THE TONGUE

If anyone among you thinks he is religious, and does not bridle his tongue but deceives his own heart, this one's religion is useless. Pure and undefiled religion before God and the Father is this: to visit orphans and widows in their trouble, and to keep oneself unspotted from the world. —James 1:26-27

To be religious in today's world is not understood to be a positive thing. Those who have religion are condemned as if it were a bad thing, even in the church. Religious people are thought to be intolerant, and the more religious a person is, the more the intolerant he is thought to be. The lack of toleration is lionized as the cause of most everything that is wrong with contemporary society. In the politically correct world, religion, rather than being the cure of immorality, is seen to the cause of the worst immorality—intolerance.

I trust that regenerate Christians are able to see through such subterfuge. Religion—true religion—is not the cause, but the cure of sin. The real intolerance in our day is not the intolerance of Christians for fellow sinners, but the intolerance of God's Word by contemporary society (sinners). And it is the most detestable intolerance because it refuses to even acknowledge the only thing that will solve the problem of intolerance—God's grace and mercy.

People today—even self-professed Christians—refuse to honor the authority of Scripture. Like the unforgivable sin of Matthew 12:31-32, they refuse to recognize the reality of God's Holy Spirit, who alone can bring sinful people into reconciliation with God. We find the same issue in Romans 2:28-29, where Paul said that the Jew who has been circumcised in the flesh but not the heart is not a true Jew.

James here does not define the whole of religion as caring for orphans and widows, but rather lifts up an essential element of practical religion. This sentence is not concerned with the inner aspects of true religion, but suggests that "an unhallowed tongue bespeaks an unhallowed heart."[1] Or as Matthew Henry observed of this verse, "If men would govern their tongues, they must govern their passions," or feelings. The mouth is a window of the heart in that it reveals the purity and/or pollution of the inner person.

The usefulness of James' admonition to "bridle the tongue" is that it can only be done by the willing submission of the heart to Christ. Like a thermometer, the tongue measures the degree of such submission. Those who fail to bridle their tongues deceive their own hearts. The lack of tongue control is a consequence of self-deception. Self-deception, then, is an enemy of true religion—and a formidable enemy it is! For there are many who fall into self-deception. We would be wise not to excuse ourselves too quickly from this disease of the soul because such excuses are the fruit of self-deception. The self-deceived are full of excuses. Many people, Christians and non-Christians alike, pride themselves on their morality.

"I'm okay on the average," they tell themselves. "Oh, I sometimes speak harshly, but for the most part I'm a pretty honest person. Sure, I've violated the Sabbath a few times—but a person has to work!" Or sometimes, "Sunday is the only day I have for myself. I don't drink or swear much, and I provide for my family."

On The Average

One day a man hired a workman to build a fence around his pasture. He lived in the country and had few cattle. He gave the workman very specific instructions about how he wanted the fence built. A few weeks later the workman brought him a bill for the fence. As he was writing out the check he engaged them in conversation.

"Did you have any materials left over?"

"'No.' the workman replied.

"That's good, the fence must be good and strong then."

"I can't say that I was able to build a perfect fence," the workman answered. "It's a pretty average fence overall. Some parts may be a little weak, but others are extra strong. There are a few gaps, but I took extra

---

1   Keddie, p. 83.

precaution to double the railing about the gaps so that the fence would be stronger in those areas. I'm sure that you will find it on the average a pretty good fence."

The man stopped writing and looked up. "You mean that you built a fence with gaps in it?" He didn't quite see the workman's point about strengthening the areas around the gaps or the benefits of an average fence. "If there's even one gap in the fence the cattle will find it and escape! Don't you know that a fence has to be completely enclosed or it's no good at all?"

"I'm not perfect," replied the workman. "I'm just an average workman. So, on the average, I think you have a pretty average fence."

The story is silly, but it illustrates the point. The effort to be a person of average morality, results in immorality (Matthew 5:48). In religion and morality, we must strive for perfection. Everything else only paves the highway to hell. Anything short of perfect obedience constitutes disobedience. Scripture demands complete obedience to God's Law. To fall short of perfect obedience is to incur the wrath of God. Anything less than a complete fence will allow the cattle to escape.

We must not deceive ourselves about this because it sets the context for the gospel of Jesus Christ, and if the context is not correctly understood, the gospel falls on deaf ears. The context is God's demand for perfect obedience to His law, the Ten Commandments. The commandments that specifically deal with the tongue are the Third—forbidding the name of the Lord to be taken in vain, and the Ninth—forbidding false witness.

These two commandments can be summarized positively by saying that we are to always speak the truth about God and others. We must speak the truth, but in order to speak the truth we must first know the truth (John 14:6). And to know the truth we must know Scripture (John 1:1). And to know Scripture we must not only study it, but we must be personally guided by God's Holy Spirit (John 8:47).

Sometimes we hear people say that the Lord led them to do this or that. I certainly believe in the providence of God, that He preserves and protects His people. God does indeed lead and guide the faithful. And yet, discerning God's will is not easy to do.

Certainly, none of us can attribute all of our decisions and actions to God's will. No one performs God's will perfectly. Not all of anyone's decisions or actions are in perfect alignment with God's will. The problem is to discern which decisions and actions can be attributed to the Lord, and which are our own. All Christians must struggle with this issue. In fact, struggling with it is what Christian living is all about.

THE SIN OF PRESUMPTION

God does indeed preserve and protect His people by leading and guiding them in very specific ways. And yet, for me to say on a regular basis that God led me here or there can be presumptuous. There is a significant difference between presumption and faith, although they also have some similarities.

Both can be bold. Paul calls Christians to be bold in the Lord (Philippians 1:14), but bold faith is different than bold presumption. To be presumptuous means to take something for granted, and God ought not be taken for granted. The sin of presumption is like hypocrisy in that it assumes the existence of something that does not exist. It assumes a relationship or a level of trust and agreement that is not a reality. Many marriages struggle with presumption. A spouse presumes some level of understanding that has never been reached. So, the one takes the other for granted, and soon the hypocrisy of their assumptions becomes intolerable.

An assumed relationship, like an assumed identity, means that it is established on false grounds. Hypocrites assume an intimacy with God that is not theirs. Too many people play at religion, pretending to traffic in godliness. They are self-deceived. Such "people draw near with their mouths And honor (God) with their lips, But have removed their hearts far from (the Lord)" (Isaiah 29:13).

Of all the sins of men, this is no doubt the most common, even in the church—especially in the church! Church people are more guilty of being presumptuous toward the Lord, than anything else. Such presumption is the deception of one's own heart. And it renders one's religion "useless" (v. 26) or vain. Such religion has no Godly affect. Where true religion requires a personal relationship with Jesus Christ, hypocrites presume such a relationship but fail to produce its fruit. They speak and pretend to love the Lord, but do not do the things that God commands. They are all talk and no walk.

Consequently, James points out two activities that are essential to true religion—charity and purity. He doesn't mean that caring for

orphans and widows is the whole of religion. There is much more to it
than this. But, while there is more, it is not true religion if it lacks these
things. In the Greek the word for *visit* is not limited to calling on
orphans and widows, but means caring for them over a period of time.
The NIV reads "look after," and is closer to the Greek.

Of course, the injunction to care for the less fortunate is easy compared to "keep(ing) oneself unspotted from the world" (v. 27). True
religion requires that we endeavor to be free from the sins of the world.
Christians are called to fence the sin of the world out of their lives. Presumptuous believers think they do a pretty good job of this—at least no
worse than anyone else, on the average. But they are self-deceived.
Thus, the first duty of the Christian according to James is to bridle the
tongue.

With that concern now in mind, James points out these two additional things that are essential to genuine faithfulness: 1) caring for the
less fortunate, and 2) sinless living. The first is not only doable, but must
be done, even though the second cannot be accomplished in this life.

Because sin free living cannot be accomplished in the flesh, it
points to the need for the righteousness of Christ. It demonstrates our
need for and dependence upon Christ. It shows us our own sinfulness,
and establishes the context for the gospel of Christ. These things are not
silly or unimportant. They are essential because they provide the setting
in which the gospel makes sense. Apart from them, the gospel of Jesus
Christ makes no sense, and is easily rejected.

WITHOUT SIN CHRIST IS UNNECESSARY

Sin provides a necessary barrier that cannot be bridged apart from
Christ. He made propitiation for our sins by His death on the cross. He
died for our salvation because we are so caught by the webs of sin that
we cannot escape without His help. Christ died to break the grip that
sin has upon all of us. And because He has done this for us, we must
then come under the authority of His Lordship for our own protection
against the continuing onslaught of sin's temptations. Only by claiming
Christ as our personal Lord and Savior—and actually endeavoring to life
our lives on the basis of Scripture—can we enjoy the mercy that He has
won for the faithful.

The confession of Christ is the tongue's true bridle. To bridle the
tongue doesn't mean to say nothing. The purpose of a bridle is to guide

or steer an animal. So it is with the tongue. God will guide the lives of the faithful by holding the reins of the tongue, which in turn steers the life of the Christian. Therefore, the faithful will employ their tongues in the praise of God. Praise on the tongue, reveals Christ in the heart. Similarly, the lack of praise reveals His absence.

WITHOUT PARTIALITY

My brethren, do not hold the faith of our Lord Jesus Christ, the Lord of glory, with partiality. For if there should come into your assembly a man with gold rings, in fine apparel, and there should also come in a poor man in filthy clothes, and you pay attention to the one wearing the fine clothes and say to him, "You sit here in a good place," and say to the poor man, "You stand there," or, "Sit here at my footstool," have you not shown partiality among yourselves, and become judges with evil thoughts?   —James 2:1-4

In chapter one James established that real Christians are faithful in both word and deed. They not only talk the faith, they walk it. They put their money where their mouths are. They apply what they learn from Scripture to their own lives. To this great principle, taught in chapter one, is now added, in chapter two, case studies of practical application.

The first case study has to do with how Christians welcome people into worship. The setting and context are obviously a worship service. And the issue is the difference in the way that rich and poor are treated. I'd like to think that this is not much of an issue for contemporary Christians, that we are beyond such gross discrimination—and to a certain extent, I think many people are beyond it. The particular situation that James dealt with is not our problem. Churches don't sanction seats of honor today, nor are some people openly and obviously discriminated against or others preferred. Things are much more subtle today.

These days partiality manifests as personal preference, and masks itself as freedom in Christ. In the church partiality is experienced as the preference of friendship over belief. Maintaining social relationships with personal friends often becomes more important than theology or concern about the particular doctrines that the Bible teaches.

That was the issue that James dealt with as well, but in James' day it manifested itself through an obvious display of giving special attention to the wealthy. Our situation is somewhat different. So, we need a contemporary example to see that the issue of partiality is still alive in the church.

Do Christians really think more highly of some people than others? You bet they do! People are partial to their friends—and naturally so. That's what friendship is all about. Friendship means treating friends in a special way. And, of course, our friends usually belong to the same social or economic class as we do. So, we find that the rich are partial to the rich and the poor are partial to the poor because rich people have rich friends and poor people have poor friends. This is only a generalization, but it is generally true.

Yet, in today's world the issue of partiality is not always related to wealth. Most churches today are composed of people of similar means. People have naturally segregated themselves into rich and poor churches so, for the most part, the dynamic that James described is not so obvious because of this self-segregating process.

Some churches have a greater socio-economic standing than others. We all know that. Hobnobbing with the rich and famous means attending certain churches. Many people attend such churches, not for theological or spiritual reasons, but for reasons of social and political status. Such churches are usually large, and have multiple staff members and dynamic programs. These churches easily conform to the Church Growth model.

When the issue of partiality comes up in our contemporary church —rich or poor—many people say that it is not their issue because they treat everyone in church the same. And to a great extent they probably do. Christians today know better than to denigrate the poor or to drool over the rich in public. So, we need to isolate the principle that James is teaching here and apply it to ourselves with greater tenacity, lest we miss the blessing of learning the lessons of impartial faithfulness.

CHRISTIAN IMPARTIALITY

The principle of impartiality means that Christian fellowship has nothing to do with worldly values or relationships. Real Christian fellowship, defined as sharing the lessons and blessings of Christian faith, is dependent upon Christ alone. Unity among Christians, the basis of Christian fellowship, must grow out of faithfulness to Christ, and nothing else. Christian fellowship must not discriminate on the basis of race, wealth, ability, social or economic status, political power, club membership, neighborhood, or friendship. Yet, to say that Christian fellowship is or should be completely indiscriminate is nonsense.

The glue of Christian fellowship must be faith alone, by the grace alone of Christ alone. Christian fellowship is not a kind of glorified friendship among Christians, although friendship develops as a natural result of fellowship. However, friendship is not a sufficient basis for Christian fellowship. The sharing of Christian beliefs and values is the essence of real fellowship.

Notice that I didn't say that fellowship assumes common beliefs and values, but that it requires the sharing of Christian beliefs and values. That means that Christian fellowship requires talking about the beliefs and values of Christ. Christian fellowship is not getting together for social events on the mere assumption of shared values, but never actually sharing them. Rather, Christian fellowship uses social gatherings as an occasion to personally share beliefs and values with others. Consequently, social gatherings where such sharing is absent are not events of Christian fellowship, but are merely social events.

For instance, two Christians go out to lunch and talk about the stuff going on at church. If they fail to share their own personal faith, their own beliefs and values, their own love and understanding of Scripture or prayer, their own struggles with the Word of God—they are not fellowshipping, they are merely socializing—and likely gossiping.

Paul set the standard for Christian fellowship. "Let no corrupt word proceed out of your mouth, but what is good for necessary edification, that it may impart grace to the hearers" (Ephesians 4:29). Edification is the root and foundation of Christian fellowship. To edify means to build, to establish, to instruct for the sake of moral and spiritual improvement.

Christian fellowship provides opportunities for edification. It differs from Christian education in that education provides a structured format, a specific lesson or agenda, where fellowship has no particular lesson, but provides for unstructured faith sharing and edification. But the bottom line is that, when there is no personal faith sharing, where people are not engaged in the edification of the saints, real fellowship does not exist.

FRIENDS, FAMILIES, OR CHRIST

Here is where contemporary Christians err with regard to James' teaching on partiality. Too many church people are united more by their personal friendships and biological families than by their commitment to Christ. Too many church people stick together, socialize together, and vote together because of family and friendship ties than because of commitment to biblical principles. And when the concerns of friends or family take precedence over commitment to the truth of Scripture, people are guilty of the kind of partiality that James is here preaching against. This situation is rampant in contemporary churches, not just in Church Growth type churches but in every type!

Matthew Henry said of this verse that conformity to Christ provides the only basis for Christian respect and fellowship. It is not that Christians are to be without respect or without common courtesy. Respect and courtesy are foundational Christian character traits. However, James teaches that respect and courtesy are never to be more important than the faithfulness of right belief, of understanding Scripture correctly, according to God's standard. We should never defer faithfulness for the sake of respect and courtesy—but that does not excuse a lack of courtesy. Rather, with all respect and courtesy we need to value faithfulness, right faithfulness, above everything else.

For instance, if some issue comes up in your church and you lend your support for or against it because your friend Joe or Sally thinks it is a good idea, you are guilty of the kind of partiality that James teaches against. You have made friendship the key element in your decision. When this kind of thing happens, church activity begins to cater to personal friendships at the expense of the gospel. Rather, each person needs to make his own biblically-based decision regarding the issue, and act upon his conscience in the light of Christ, without regard for the particular personalities involved. If you can't do that, it would be better to do nothing. The key, of course, is making biblically-based decisions in the light of Christ.

For most churches, the ostensible purpose of church votes is to discern and reveal God's will regarding a particular matter. So, if you are not sure what God's will is, it is better not to vote at all than to vote for something you know is less than God's will, i.e., your friend's opinion. (The same principle applies to political elections, by the way.) The partiality of friendships and politics quickly obscures God's will in any church. This is the issue that James is concerned with. The issue is much deeper than simply being polite to poor people. The issue is the very human tendency to be guided by worldly concerns of sociability and acceptability, rather than by Christ alone through Scripture.

James uses the example of the way that rich and poor are welcomed into church, but many other examples can be used. The principle is "do not hold the faith...with partiality" (NKJV), or "as believers...don't show favoritism (NIV), or "have not the faith...with respect of persons" (v. 1-2—KJV). Don't let friendships or personalities obscure your commitment to Christ, but maintain your commitment to the truth of Scripture above everything else.

CHRISTIAN UNITY

The unity of any church must be, then, not personal friendships, nor social standing in the community, but the abiding truth of Scripture—doctrine. The word *doctrine* is not very popular today, but it simply means principles, tenets, or beliefs. It is the content of teaching or the substance of understanding. Doctrine is "what the Bible teaches." Every church and every denomination teaches something about the Bible. Whatever it teaches is its doctrine. Even a church that claims to be nondoctrinal teaches the doctrine that there are no significant biblical principles worth teaching.

Today there is a great hue and cry that "doctrine divides." Therefore, the argument goes, the church must set aside doctrine for the sake of unity. People believe that they need to go along in order to get along. But the truth is that real biblical unity is always a function of doctrinal unity. Biblical unity is unity that is based upon what the Bible teaches. All other unity is based upon partiality, upon personalities and relationships.

The issue for faithful Christians and their churches is not whether or not to teach doctrine, but what particular doctrine to teach. In churches where there is freedom for the development of personal understanding of Scripture, the only solution to this doctrinal concern is for the church to teach the classic, historical doctrines of our origins—in our case, Protestant, Reformed doctrine.

It should be noted, of course, that the classic Protestant Reformed teaching involves the recovery the original intent of the Bible as a whole—Old Testament and New. Such teaching, then, provides the foundation for the free development of personal, but informed faith, faith informed by the tradition of Old Testament and New Testament saints who have preceded us. Add to these biblical saints all of the Christian saints who have preceded us as well, and you begin to see the wealth of information and testimony that is included in the classic Protestant Reformed tradition. Of course, the non-biblical writings are not perfect, but we must understand them correctly before we can refine or even disagree with them.

Christ is the Rock upon which the Church is founded. That is not the issue. The issue is, "What does the Bible teach about faithfulness and the nature and structure of Christ's church?" Clearly, Protestant churches teach neither Roman Catholic nor Eastern Orthodox doctrine. Protestant churches should teach the doctrines of the Protestant Reformation. Unfortunately many Christians, even those belonging to historically Reformed churches, do not know much about the real concerns of the Protestant Reformation.

Nonetheless, it is upon that foundation that Scripture allows for a degree of freedom of belief and understanding with regard to particular issues. Ours is not a cookie-cutter faith. Yet, without the foundation of Reformed Protestant doctrine, people are unable to correctly believe anything for themselves. People must know the biblical and historical basics in order to differ from anyone else intelligently. Therefore, the responsibility of Protestant churches is to teach the classic Protestant Reformed fundamentals of the faith.

What has happened in the Modern era is that the denominations have concerned themselves with teaching their particular denominational distinctives and have failed to teach the foundational principles of the faith. The result has been the deterioration of foundational faithfulness, and a weakening of both the churches and the Christians who inhabit them.

Church unity rests upon the belief that without the fundamentals of the Christian faith the truth of Scripture is hopelessly obscured by human tradition—in particular the traditions of Roman Catholicism and

Eastern Orthodoxy. However, the Reformed churches are just as susceptible to succumbing to human tradition as the others—and in many ways have already done so![1] If people cannot agree in this, they cannot even call themselves Christian, much less Protestant. Without an historic faith foundation people and their churches become uninformed sects, not historical Christian churches.

And yet, it is our own partiality toward family and friends that often causes concern about and rejection of such classic, fundamental doctrines. Teaching the fundamentals of Reformed Protestantism causes concern for the salvation and well-being—not only of ourselves, but of our Catholic, Orthodox, and Pagan (unchurched) friends and family members. More often than not, the issue that divides people concerns who is actually saved and how they are saved. Historically it is known as the doctrine of election.

The concern here is not to dwell on such issues, but to point out the fact that the fundamentals of Protestant belief must be taught for the sake of faithfulness to biblical truth. It is not a matter of personal preference, not a matter of my opinion or yours. It is a matter of what Scripture actually teaches. The elimination of biblical doctrines or teaching requires the elimination of historical, biblical truth itself.

The temptation to hold the faith with partiality in our day is this matter of ignoring our responsibility to teach biblical doctrine for the sake of maintaining harmony among family and friends (Matthew 10:34-39). It is a very real concern and in most churches it has already interfered with the fundamental commitments and responsibilities of church members. That is to say that church people often favor family and friends over biblical truth. Where a conflict arises between Scripture and family and/or friends, people often choose the latter over the former for the sake of harmony in the home and at church.

But when people do that they undermine the foundation of Christ's life and ministry. A faulty understanding of Christ and His church that is not firmly grounded in the historic reality of His life and mission as described in the Bible and taught in the historic creeds and confessions is not Christian belief at all. It is the stuff of "profane and old wives' fables" (1 Timothy 4:7), not historic Christianity.

---

1   See *Conflict of Ages—The Great Debate of the Moral Relations of God and Man*, Edward Beecher, D. D., Phillip A. Ross, editor, Pilgrim Platform, Marietta, Ohio, 1853, 2012. I was not aware of Beecher when this was originally written.

Christians cannot abandon the historic faith without abandoning Christian faith. Christians cannot honor friends and family more than the right understanding of Christ's atoning sacrifice. Does the Bible put Jesus above family and friends? Jesus said,

> "everyone who has left houses or brothers or sisters or father or mother or wife or children or lands, for My name's sake, shall receive a hundred-fold, and inherit eternal life" (Matthew 19:29).

This is Christian faith without partiality for family or friends.

Christ died for the faithful. Christ died for the sake of God's truth, for the sake of right understanding and right doctrine. He gave His life rather than renege on His understanding of the faith. To abandon doctrine, to abandon what the Bible teaches is to abandon Christ Himself. He not only died for the forgiveness of sins, He died for our right to believe the truth without partiality or favoritism, without error or fear.

In Christ we must abandon the pettiness of personal preference and partiality, and boldly proclaim with a united voice the unvarnished truth of Jesus Christ—Creator, Redeemer, Lord, and Savior of the world!

MERCY FOR THE GUILTY

Listen, my beloved brethren: Has God not chosen the poor of this world to be rich in faith and heirs of the kingdom which He promised to those who love Him? But you have dishonored the poor man. Do not the rich oppress you and drag you into the courts? Do they not blaspheme that noble name by which you are called? If you really fulfill the royal law according to the Scripture, "You shall love your neighbor as yourself," you do well; but if you show partiality, you commit sin, and are convicted by the law as transgressors. For whoever shall keep the whole law, and yet stumble in one point, he is guilty of all. For He who said, "Do not commit adultery," also said, "Do not murder." Now if you do not commit adultery, but you do murder, you have become a transgressor of the law. So speak and so do as those who will be judged by the law of liberty. For judgment is without mercy to the one who has shown no mercy. Mercy triumphs over judgment. —James 2:5-13*

J ames continues with his case study of how Christians are to treat the rich and the poor. The principle he teaches is that God recognizes no such differences. Salvation is not a matter of wealth or poverty. It's not that God doesn't know the difference between wealth and poverty, but as James goes on to teach, from God's perspective worldly wealth is more a snare than a blessing. Wealth tends to pull human attention away from God.

He states the principle by pointing out that "God (has) chosen the poor of this world to be rich in faith and heirs of the kingdom which He promised to those who love Him" (v. 5). Again, it is not that God chooses to save or bless all poor people, but that His blessings cut across the human categories of rich and poor, as if such categories don't matter. And they don't! God's blessings are a function of His grace, not human categories. God values His kingdom more than wealth or poverty, so even the poor who are saved are rich beyond all worldly measures.

This is an important teaching because it means that grace and salvation are available to absolutely anyone, from any walk of life, regardless of any limitations that we might want to apply. Because salvation is by grace through faith, because it is a matter of God's choosing, God's doing, salvation is available to anyone without regard for the human concerns of wealth, position, character, deeds, or anything else. This is the heart of the good news of the gospel. God chooses people from every possible walk of life, without regard for what we might think is important—wealth, position, character, or deeds. Grace means that the conditions of salvation are in God's hands alone.

For that we can be grateful because just as we might want to exclude some people from salvation, so others might want to exclude us. Whereas, for the most part, the exclusions that God makes are those who exclude themselves. And don't kid yourself, there are many people who want nothing to do with God's salvation. Of course, some people misunderstand God and salvation, and because of their misunderstanding they think they want it, and may even think that they already have it. But when they discover the truth about God and salvation, which always involves the doctrine of election—the fact that God chooses His disciples (Matthew 20:16, John 15:16), they turn and walk away.

James' point here is that when we treat the poor as if they have no right to God's grace we dishonor, not only them, but more importantly, we dishonor God. To refuse God's grace ourselves, or to refuse those whom God has blessed—rich or poor—is to refuse God's authority. And ultimately, the dishonor of God's authority amounts to a refusal of His gospel.

James drives the point home by reminding Christians that if they are going to play favorites, they really ought to favor the poor because it is the people with worldly means who continually oppress and employ various measures against others for the sake of gaining even more wealth. "No," said James, "if God were partial, which He is not, He would prefer the poor to the rich." James pressed the point in order to convict his listeners, to demonstrate to them that they were guilty of breaking God's law. He was not concerned about offending them, he was concerned that they had offended God, and deserved God's wrath because of it.

> "If you really fulfill the royal law according to the Scripture,
> 'You shall love your neighbor as yourself,' you do well; but if
> you show partiality, you commit sin, and are convicted by the
> law as transgressors" (v. 8-9).

James' purpose here was to demonstrate that they were guilty before the law. We cannot understand James' point unless we also understand and personally experience the universal condemnation of God's law. We must feel the error of our own ways, our own favoritism, the fact that we so willingly prefer to honor our friends and families above God's Word and the particular things that it teaches.

THE TWO SIDES OF PREJUDICE

A black Christian had taken a new job and moved to a new city. In that city he began visiting churches. At some point he finally decided to join a church near the hospital where he was a medical doctor in residency. After worship one day he asked the pastor about becoming a member of the church.

The pastor knew that he had been well received as a visitor, but that his request for membership would not set well with the board. The church was in a suburban neighborhood and had a narrow opinion of blacks. Not wanting to deal with the issue, the pastor asked him to pray about it for a couple of weeks, "to be sure of God's will in the matter." After a couple of weeks the pastor asked the man about his prayers.

"How is God guiding you in the matter of church membership?" he inquired.

"Well, sir," the black man responded, "God told me that He has been trying to get into this church for the past fifteen years and He hasn't succeeded. So God advised me that I had better not go where He has not been welcomed."

Prejudice is a kind of partiality. Race is a another human category that does not enter into God's consideration of grace and salvation.

Again, the nature and abundance of God's grace suggests that people are included or excluded from the body of Christ only by the prerogative of the Holy Spirit. While it does not belong to the decisions of men to *exclude* anyone from church membership, neither does it belong to men to *include* anyone. Our job, as in everything, is to agree with the Holy Spirit.

People today generally understand the principle of negative prejudice, in the sense of exclusion of membership. More difficult for many people is the matter of violating God's will by erring on the side of positive prejudice. Here, the error is made by granting church membership on the basis of friendship or family relationship, or some other human category.

But extending membership (and thereby implying that a person is saved because he is a member of a church) on the basis of friendship or family ties is just as offensive to God as excluding membership for some human reason. We are not free to exclude membership because someone is black (or any particular race), or because they are poor, or because they belong to the wrong political party, or live on the wrong side of town, etc. We know these things all too well.

But the other side of the prejudice coin is that we are not free to extend membership to anyone on the basis of anything except biblical criteria—personal belief and repentance that result from new birth in Christ. We are not free to welcome people into membership just because we know them or like them. Our knowing someone has nothing to do with God's grace. Here is where the church has erred repeatedly and significantly over the past fifty years—maybe more.

Speaking of faithful Christians, Jesus said, "You will know them by their fruits" (Matthew 7:16). Consequently, the fruits of the Spirit are God's measure of a renewed heart and, therefore, are the required measurement for church membership. In the world, knowing the right people means a lot, but in the church it means nothing. The only person in the church worth knowing is Jesus Christ. And the only way that we can know that someone knows Christ is by the fruit of the Spirit in their lives, "love, joy, peace, long-suffering, kindness, goodness, faithfulness" (Galatians 5:22).

To extend membership on any other criteria is not kindness or even toleration, but outright sinfulness. James said, "if you show partiality, you commit sin" (v. 9). And Paul said, "the wages of sin is death" (Romans 6:23). We are not free to determine membership qualifications for ourselves. Rather, we must discern the presence or absence of the Holy Spirit in a person's life based upon the fruits of the Spirit. We must follow God's lead. To be too lenient in this regard is just as much a sin as being too strict.

THE LAW OF LIBERTY

For the second time James makes reference to the "law of liberty' (James 1:25 & James 2:12). What a jarring juxtaposition of terms that is! He calls the gospel the "law of liberty," differentiating it from the Old Testament law. James does not oppose freedom (or liberty) against law, but suggests that real freedom requires willing submission to God's law, and that real obedience to the law must be freely given. Upon conversion Christians should *want* to obey God's law, not because they must, but because they believe it to be the best option available. God's law provides the only real freedom. And conversely, freedom in Christ brings with it the personal desire to obey God's law.

James said again that to fail in any point of obedience is to fail to obey the whole law. Anything short of perfect obedience constitutes a failure to obey. The purpose of God's law is to cause human failure, to demonstrate the limits of human ability. The purpose of the law is to demonstrate our sin to us, to prove that we are sinners through and through. Every Christian must personally feel the weight of God's judgment. Every Christian must come to the point of personal conviction because there is no repentance without conviction, and there is no salvation without repentance.

The thing that is so uncomfortable about such biblical preaching is that the preacher will not let the listeners off the hook of condemnation by the law. Scripture itself pounds relentlessly on this point. All are guilty before God, and God is a just judge. As uncomfortable as it may be, it is a necessary fact. It's part of our history. The universal reality of sin sets up the right reception of the gospel. Yet, the truth of sin is not to be believed because is makes the gospel meaningful, but because it is itself factually true.

People who don't like the fire and brimstone of the Old Testament are right in their assessment of such preaching. The law is a harsh taskmaster. But the truth is that God's wrath is hanging over us like a hammer over an anvil, ready to strike a blow for justice, a blow that is long overdue. It's not so much the ranting and raving that people don't like. Ranters and ravers always put on a good show. Popular evangelicalism has long known that.

The thing that really troubles thoughtful people is the reality of the severity of God's law. And the old time preacher won't—can't—let anyone off the hook. He drives home the point of sin and depravity again and again, not because he enjoys making people uncomfortable, but because it is the truth of the human condition. So, where is the good news in all of this?

THE GOOD NEWS FOLLOWS THE BAD

The good news is that there is mercy in Christ, but only *in Christ*. The good news is that Christ has come. Mercy is available. Jesus Christ offers the mercy of forgiveness and reconciliation—not because of anything that you or I have done, but because of God's overwhelming love. The only release from the tension of the conviction of sin brought about by God's law is salvation in Jesus Christ.

It is the preacher's job to *proclaim* it to everyone, but no preacher can *give* it. The Holy Spirit alone gives it. The preacher only proclaims it. The preacher can only invite people to come to Christ and lay their burdens at His feet. The preacher can only share Christ's proclamation of salvation. But no preacher, no church or denomination can give it. Only Christ gives salvation. Only the Holy Spirit can provide the necessary reconciliation. People must come to Christ and receive it. People must receive what is given. But no preacher or church can give it. It's not theirs to give.

The error that so many preachers make is to give premature assurance of pardon to individual sinners, or to suggest that people are in fact saved. No preacher or priest or church or denomination or evangelist can assure you of your personal salvation. That is not their job. It is beyond their knowledge and authority. Rather, *you* must wrest that assurance from the Holy Spirit yourself. Like Jacob of old, you must wrestle with God. It is God who gives personal assurance of salvation. You must take it up with Him.

You can easily fool me about your heart. Preachers are an easy mark. Christians want to trust people, and more so pastors are trusting. You can just as easily fool yourself. Self-deception is Satan's favorite tool. But you can't fool God. He knows when conviction and repentance are real, so He provides personal assurance of salvation at the appropriate time.

There is an order in God's kingdom, and an order to His ways. Following conviction, repentance, and salvation, personal assurance of faith can then be gained by engaging the disciplines of the faith. Assurance of faith is the result of an actual, ongoing, tried-and-true relationship with Jesus Christ through His means of grace—worship, prayer, study, fellowship, service, etc. Assurance, like trust, is earned, not bestowed.

As one begins walking in the strength of Christ, the strength of one's walk begins to conform more and more to God's will. The renewal of the mind through immersion in Scripture increases conformity to Christ and decreases conformity to the world. Before long such spiritual growth blossoms into an unshakable personal assurance of faith.

The point is that the blessings can't come unless and until the storms of sin and guilt water the seeds of conviction and repentance. Everyone wants the blessings of salvation, but few are willing to endure the trials of conviction and repentance. People just want to be personally assured that they are okay with God.

But that's not something that preachers can give. Personal assurance of salvation is very real and very available. But it comes from the Lord, not the preacher. It is yours for the asking, but you must ask. It is the preacher's to proclaim, but it is yours to receive.

You must come to the Lord. Trust Him, He is just and merciful. We are all hurtling down the highway of hell and nothing but the intervention of Jesus Christ can stop us from reaching that intended destination.

> "God... is rich in mercy, because of His great love with which He loved us, even when we were dead in trespasses, made us alive together with Christ (by grace you have been saved), and raised us up together, and made us sit together in the heavenly places in Christ Jesus, that in the ages to come He might show the exceeding riches of His grace in His kindness toward us in Christ Jesus" (Ephesians 2:4-7).

Come to the Lord for He is just and merciful.

Have you really been saved? Are you washed in the blood of the Lamb? Do you have personal assurance of faith?

Take the next step. Come to Christ and receive the assurance of your faith.

Hollow Testimony

*What does it profit, my brethren, if someone says he has faith but
does not have works? Can faith save him? If a brother or sister is
naked and destitute of daily food, and one of you says to them,
"Depart in peace, be warmed and filled," but you do not give them
the things which are needed for the body, what does it profit? Thus
also faith by itself, if it does not have works, is dead.*

—James 2:14-17

In James we find what at first seems to contradict Paul's teaching
regarding salvation by faith alone. Paul said, "For by grace you have
been saved through faith, and that not of yourselves" (Ephesians
2:8). And James concludes in verse 24 a theme that begins in the verses
above, "You see then that a man is justified by works, and not by faith
only." Here is a classic dichotomy that fills thousands of pages of theology. What is the proper relationship between faith and works?

James was not concerned with mere theory. He was a practical man
who said that people's deeds ought to be consistent with their words. If a
person says that he is generous or kind, he ought to demonstrate generosity or kindness. James' concern was simple and straightforward. Integrity of character must find expression in both conversation and
action.

James' points to the problem of self-deception. Only the most hardened degenerates knowingly misrepresent themselves. People like thinking of themselves as good and honest. People generally believe themselves to actually be what they think they are. But the truth is not so
simple, says James. People are more likely to deceive themselves than to
know themselves truly.

The deception happens when people either redefine the meaning of the word *good* by changing the definition to fit their behavior, or they simply ignore those behaviors that contradict their positive self-description. It is a kind of denial. People don't consciously ignore things, they simply forget about them. They don't pay attention to them. They overlook them.

For example, consider those who redefine the word *good* in order to fit the term to their own behavior. Perhaps the accessible and widely abused—and therefore the most convicting—example has to do with the Seventh Commandment, "You shall not commit adultery" (Exodus 20:14).

REDEFINING GOOD

While technically the term *adultery* means being sexually unfaithful to one's own spouse, people often ignore its broader application which includes fornication—sexual activity among unmarried people. People rationalize, "I'm not married. So, this law does not apply to me. I'm free to experiment, to date, to be sexually active, to play the field until I decide to marry." People redefine adultery and fornication to mean something that they themselves do not do, so that it indicates some perversion worse than their own.

Today we have children following in the footsteps—even standing on the shoulders—of their free-love, baby-boomer parents. Whatever sexual perversions their parents were involved in are considered mere child's play by their now grown children. In addition, most entertainment stars are blatant fornicators. A major media industry has arisen just to track their indiscretions. Even President Bill Clinton has engaged in sexual perversity—and every child in America knows it! It is common today. It is the social norm. Yet, people still believe themselves to be basically *good*.

Over the last few decades the authorities of our society have utterly redefined what is sexually acceptable. Landlords cannot discriminate against cohabiting couples. Parents and grandparents authorize the fornication of cohabitation by a conspiracy of silence. The American Association of Psychologists have downgraded (reclassified) several previously aberrant sexual behaviors from psychological deviations that once required treatment. They are now acceptable alternatives of sexual expression that no longer require treatment. What was once medically considered to be pathological behavior, is now considered to be normal by the medical establishment. The redefinition of *normal* has effected the definition of *good*.

Contemporary culture has redefined morality and goodness so that people won't see themselves as the sinners they are. People think of themselves as being good, where *good* is defined as average or normal. But where good has become average, the standard of measurement has degraded significantly. Over time the average moral behavior of contemporary people—including many professing Christians—has degenerated into blatant biblical immorality. It is easy for children to be confused about sexuality. Nonetheless, it is clear from Scripture that God forbids all sexual activity outside of marriage. Period.

DENIAL

The other way that self-deception operates is through denial, by ignoring those behaviors that contradict a person's self-image or self-understanding. Denial operates where people simply refuse to recognize a fact. A husband who ignores the unhappiness of his wife and family is in denial. A man who disregards the warning of his doctor to quit smoking or drinking or eating certain foods is in denial. When facts are ignored, denial is in operation.

The Bible speaks of denial as a kind of blindness. Jesus described the Pharisees as

> "Blind guides, who strain out a gnat and swallow a camel! Woe to you, scribes and Pharisees, hypocrites! For you cleanse the outside of the cup and dish, but inside they are full of extortion and self-indulgence. Blind Pharisee, first cleanse the inside of the cup and dish, that the outside of them may be clean also" (Matthew 23:24-26).

The Pharisees in Jesus' time were consumed with denial.

The Pharisees were men of eminent spiritual testimonies, but whose behaviors denied the very faith to which they testified. We think of them as being spiritually blind because they could not see that their lives were not in conformity with their testimony. That is the problem that James' here describes. And the problem also belongs to us.

The old country preacher used to say that there are two parts to the gospel. The first is believing it, the second is behaving it. The two halves make a whole, but either half by itself is not the gospel.

Preserved To Death

An English merchant once presented a tribal king in the heart of Africa with a gift. He gave him a sundial. The king didn't know what a sundial was, but he knew it was valuable. So, he built a house for it to keep it safe. But in the shade of the house the sundial could no longer serve its purpose. The king rendered it useless by trying to protect it.

That's how many people treat their faith. They enclose it within the walls and stained glass windows of a church building. Worse yet are those who wall off their faith from their own lives. They treasure the faith in their hearts, but never actually live it out. They own a Bible, but never actually read it. They praise the goodness of God's Word, but never actually engage it. They honor it with one hand and deny it with the other.

We see the same kind of thing played out at the national level. On the Fourth of July we celebrate America's Independence Day. We honor the founding of America and what we have come to know as American freedom. But our celebration has become hollow and hypocritical. Today we stand at the edge of history looking back on the fading greatness of America.

The glory of America is celebrated in her founding document, the Constitution of the United States. That document was written by godly men—not all were Christian, but nearly all ostensibly respected biblical values. The Constitution itself is not a Christian document. It does not mention Christ, but it is a great document in the sense that it was grounded on some of the best of the biblical traditions of Old Testament law and New Testament freedom in Christ. It was a product of the Protestant Work Ethic, of biblical values, and godly men.

But without Christ, without Scripture, it never would have been. Such a document would be unthinkable without its biblical foundation. Such a country as the United States of America could not have arisen, but for the biblical character of her founding people. I don't mean that every American is or was a saved Christian. I only mean that the general character of Americans has been significantly shaped by biblical values. Americans have never completely embodied biblical values, but the fact that we have been positively effected by biblical values cannot be denied.

For two hundred years America was a biblically informed nation— neither perfectly nor completely, but significantly. Her European immigrants brought their Christianity with them. They brought their biblical values and their desire to make America great and good. For two centuries immigrants followed in the footsteps of the founders, seeking religious and political freedom, and a better life—not all, but a great many.

However, over the past several decades we have witnessed the systematic gutting of America. Beginning in the 1960s the underbelly of America's biblical values was ripped open by the demands for ever-greater freedoms. What began as a vision of religious freedom and self-government based upon biblical principles culminated in the demand for absolute personal freedom—the freedom to pursue self-desire at any cost. The biblical morals that had governed the American experiment were thrown off by the children of her abundant success. In a single generation the laws that once protected the biblical values of America were inverted, and now protect Americans *from* biblical values.

Greatness always stands on the shoulders of her predecessors. America's greatness has for centuries stood on the shoulders of the Judeo-Christian history that gave her birth. But today the laws of the land are no longer shaped by the values of Judeo-Christian history, but are more and more being shaped by the godless values of Hollywood, Wall Street, and Karl Marx. Lust and greed manipulate and seduce Americans more and more with every passing day. Marxism, disguised as many other things—mostly as Humanism, reigns in American universities. These values often replace the values our children learn at church, thus undermining both society and church.

While the majority of Americans have not completely succumbed to lust, greed, and democratic socialism, these deconstructed values, have refashioned our best schools and universities, and are being broadcast daily far and wide by the most advanced technology the world has ever seen. The acidity of lust and greed are corroding the foundations of the American experiment beyond recognition. Full-blown degradation will soon swallow the American experiment unless these self-destructive tendencies are soon neutralized by an outpouring of the Holy Spirit. There is no other neutralizing factor.

Our current national crisis is not a crisis of patriotism, nor of education, nor economics, nor politics, nor ecology, but is a crisis of faith. The national deterioration that is evident everywhere has little to do with the growing diversity of American culture and much to do with the failing faith of individual Americans. We stand on the brink of a new millennium. Like Joshua at the crossing of the Jordan our millennium crossing brings us face to face with the promises of God. And what are the biblical promises of God? To bless the faithful and to curse the unfaithful (Deuteronomy 28).

God said to the Israelites of old and says to us today,

> "'I have given you a land for which you did not labor, and cities which you did not build, and you dwell in them; you eat of the vineyards and olive groves which you did not plant.' Now therefore, fear the Lord, serve Him in sincerity and in truth, and put away the gods (lust and greed) which your fathers served on the other side of the River and in Egypt. Serve the Lord! And if it seems evil to you to serve the Lord, choose for yourselves this day whom you will serve, whether the gods which your fathers served that were on the other side of the River, or the gods of the Amorites, in whose land you dwell. But as for me and my house, we will serve the Lord" (Joshua 24:13-15).

We, too, must choose whom we will serve: the gods of lust and greed that have saturated American culture with their degenerate slime, or the God of Jesus Christ who alone stands opposed to the glitz and kitsch of contemporary godlessness.

However, it will not do in our day to engage in great orgies of religious testimony. It is not signs and wonders that we need, but the hard Rock of repentance and conversion. If we only proclaim an experience or new understanding of God's Word, but fail to have our hardened hearts broken by the grace of repentance and the conviction of personal sin, we will only add to our sins the self-deception described in this second chapter of James. Unless our sinful lives change and we give ourselves completely to the government of the Holy Spirit, the grand history of the American Empire will only serve as a monument to the sinfulness of man and the veracity of God's promise to punish disobedience. And even that will serve God's glory!

Christ died for our sins. Christ died so that salvation would be available in *this* moment of history. Christ died so that God's Word would prove true, that He would bless the faithful and curse the faithless. Your life will testify to the steadfastness of God's promises. God will be glorified by your faithfulness, or by your unfaithfulness. God's truth and righteousness will be proven faithful either way.

You can come to God's judgment kicking and screaming, or you can come of your own free will, protected by the blood and advocacy of Jesus Christ. But you will come to the bench of God's judgment.

Do You Want to Know?

But someone will say, "You have faith, and I have works." Show me your faith without your works, and I will show you my faith by my works. You believe that there is one God. You do well. Even the demons believe—and tremble! But do you want to know, O foolish man, that faith without works is dead? Was not Abraham our father justified by works when he offered Isaac his son on the altar? Do you see that faith was working together with his works, and by works faith was made perfect? And the Scripture was fulfilled which says, "Abraham believed God, and it was accounted to him for righteousness." And he was called the friend of God. You see then that a man is justified by works, and not by faith only. Likewise, was not Rahab the harlot also justified by works when she received the messengers and sent them out another way? For as the body without the spirit is dead, so faith without works is dead also.

—*James 2:18-26*

James was clearly correcting a misunderstanding about the nature of Christian faith. Most of the epistles (letters) in the New Testament do the same thing. They are not mere statements and testimonies of positive faith, but are intended to correct the misunderstandings held by many of the early Christians.

The issue under scrutiny here is the relationship between faith and works. James said that faith requires more than testimony, more than mere words. It requires behavior that is consistent with Christian testimony. James was correcting a misunderstanding about Paul's teaching of justification by faith alone, which was not unique to Paul, but runs throughout the Bible. Paul taught that people cannot earn their way to

71

heaven, and James taught that God's justification by the mercy of His free grace necessarily results in good and godly behavior. Again, the behavior is not required for justification, but is the consequence of justification.

When James said that "even the demons believe—and tremble" (v. 19) he indicated part of the misunderstanding he intended to correct. That misunderstanding produced an empty faith or vain belief, a kind of verbal or emotional assent to Christ (or God) that is all talk and no walk. He suggests that there was a kind of Christian belief being practiced that was false because it had no real connection to salvation. James said that in spite of the fact that some people confessed belief in Christ, their belief was empty.

The Greek word is *phrisso*. It was a New Testament figure of speech that indicated a strong emotional reaction. It has been translated as *tremble* or *shudder*. When James said that "the demons believe—and tremble" (v. 20) he invoked the image of a powerful emotional reaction to the Word of God. No doubt such a reaction might be accompanied by tears and tremors, a violent shaking of the limbs or body. People could even fall down or faint. Surely their words would be emotionally laden, even stuttering, stammering, and otherwise confused with incomplete sentences, half thoughts, and involuntary expressions of raw emotion. If you have ever seen people at the scene of an accident, you know what James means.

"Nothing wrong with that," said James. That kind of thing happens all the time. Often repentance and conviction overflow with uncontrollable emotions of fear, remorse, and sorrow. Certainly, some sort of emotional response to God's grace is a normal and necessary part of conversion.

"But," says James, "it is not enough."

James' point was that the demons have the same reaction. Emotions don't produce saving faith. An emotional reaction to God is necessary, but not sufficient. Sometimes the emotional reaction is not discernible to an outside observer. Many people prefer to keep their feelings to themselves. Nonetheless, there is always some emotional engagement of Christ that accompanies salvation. That emotion is often at the heart of human motivation.

Yet, there is much more to salvation than emotional response. Christian motivation is more than emotion. Genuine faith is both intel-

lectual and visceral. Biblical faith requires a particular object of belief
and produces objective knowledge, where objective knowledge is simply knowledge that can be shared to produce a common understanding.
What sets people free is the truth—not mere knowledge about Jesus
Christ. Knowing how He lived and died is one thing, but knowing
Him as Lord and Savior is something entirely different. James was talking, as am I, about the relationship developed through knowing Christ
personally.

Knowledge of God, which will produce an emotional reaction of
some degree, is necessary. But if one's relationship with Christ is real,
then it will also result in changed behavior and good deeds. A requisite
change of behavior must follow. It is this change of attitude and behavior that then proves or justifies a person in the eyes of God's people
gathered in fellowship. The love of God and the desire to serve Him are
readily seen among the people of God.

A RESULT NOT A REQUIREMENT

James does not argue that people are saved by doing good works or
by believing the right things, but that saved people—people already
saved by the grace of God—do good works and believe the right things.
"Faith without works is dead" (v. 20). Testimony without evidence is
worthless. Talking the talk without walking the walk is jive!

James cites the example of Abraham, who offered to sacrifice his
son, Isaac. James said that Abraham was "justified by works when he
offered Isaac his son on the altar" (v. 21). Isaac was born in Genesis 21:2,
but Abraham "believed God, and it was accounted to him for righteousness" (v. 23), as James pointed out, in Genesis 15:6. The point is
that Abraham's justification occurred six chapters and fifteen years
before Isaac was born, which means that James' use of the word *justification* did not apply to God's justification of Abraham, but to Abraham's
justification or proof (manifestation) of His faith. Abraham's faith was
proven by his willingness to sacrifice Isaac, even though God had justified Abraham many years before. James said that "by works faith was
made complete" (v. 22), or proven, established, even tempered.

What was true for Abraham is true for all of God's people throughout time. Salvation is the result of God's free grace alone. God credits
the work of Jesus Christ to the account of particular sinners—those
whom He has regenerated—for His own reasons. It is as if God deposits

money (credit) in a person's bank account and then asks the person to agree that Christ is indeed his personal Lord and Savior. Christians who so agree then draw on that credit as they do what Christ would have them do. That line of credit is necessary in order to do God's will. God's will can only be done where such a line of credit has already been extended because people cannot afford of their own resources to do the will of God.

To get a line of credit in God's books requires God's prior justification and an acknowledgment of its receipt. Salvation actually begins as an accounting procedure in God's ledger. We don't do it, God does it. He's the accountant. The records are His. He makes the entries. We receive the grace. We receive the credit for Christ's righteousness. But God is the keeper of the books, and He Himself makes all the entries.

Think about banking. When we say "deposit this amount in my name" or "withdraw this amount in my name" we mean deposit or withdraw it from the person's account. If I write you a check and you take it to the bank and cash it, the money is withdrawn from my account because my name is on the check. But if you believe that my check is worthless and don't cash it, or for any reason you fail to cash it, it is indeed worthless to you. My check is valuable to you only if it has your name on it, and you can prove that you are who you say you are, and you have enough faith in me to actually cash it. Only then do you in fact receive its value, or have it credited to your account.

So it is with God. God has the resources that you need. He is Life and Light. He has more than enough salvation for all of His people. Christ has already died for the sins of His people. His righteousness has already been credited to the appropriate accounts. God's check has already been written,

> "just as He chose us in Him before the foundation of the world,
> that we should be holy and without blame before Him in love,
> having predestined us to adoption as sons by Jesus Christ to
> Himself, according to the good pleasure of His will, to the praise
> of the glory of His grace, by which He has made us accepted in
> the Beloved. In Him we have redemption through His blood,
> the forgiveness of sins, according to the riches of His grace"
> (Ephesians 1:4-7).

It is as if your great uncle won the lottery, died, and willed it to you with the single provision that you spend it according to his will. It's yours on the condition that you abide by the terms of the will. You are free to determine the details regarding how it is spent and to enjoy it. All you need to do is go the bank and prove who you are.

Receiving the inheritance requires more than just believing that it is yours. You must present yourself at the bank, and you must prove your identity. If you don't claim it or if you can't prove your identity, then your belief in is vain. It is useless. You can't withdraw the money just because you think it belongs to you. This is what James means by "a man is justified by works, and not by faith only" (v. 23). Salvation belongs only to God's people, who always produce works of righteousness. Of course, Christians do not do works of righteousness in order to gain personal merit or salvation. Rather, they do them in thankfulness for the merit of Jesus Christ that has been given to them out of the grace and mercy of God's love alone.

RAHAB'S WORKS

Secondly, James calls on the story of Rahab the harlot to prove his point. The story of Rahab begins in Joshua 2. Moses had died and Joshua was planning a military campaign against Jericho as directed by God. Spies were sent to Jericho to assess the situation. They lodged with Rahab, probably because she was a prostitute, which would provide a cover story should people become suspicious about why they were there. Strange men would have been in and out of her place all the time. The fact of her prostitution provided good cover—a reason for them to be in Jericho, and a cover against suspicion.

Nonetheless, the king discovered that they were spies and sent the police to arrest them. The police surrounded the house and called for their surrender. But Rahab lied to the police, saying that the spies had just left, and if they were quick they might still catch them. The police took the bait and hurried after them.

Rahab had hidden the spies on her roof because she wanted to make a deal with them. God had revealed to her that Jericho would be defeated. She testified to the spies that Jericho would fall because of "the Lord your God, He is God in heaven above and on earth beneath" (Joshua 2:11). She confessed her faith that God was also Lord of her life, and of her city, and she entered into a covenant with the spies by a mutual oath to the Lord.

She asked them to spare her family during the conquest because she had spared them from the Jericho police. The spies agreed that a life for a life was a fair deal. Rahab identified her home by hanging a scarlet rope or sash from her window. By that identification her house was spared during the siege.

When James said that Rahab was justified by her works he meant that she had proven loyal to God by her works. Rahab's works had been to hide the spies, and while her works preceded her salvation in the temporal sense regarding the battle of Jericho, her spiritual justification by God had precedence. She established her faith, her prior justification by God, when she lied to the police about the spies. Rahab was part of God's plan to conquer Jericho. Her spiritual justification was part of God's plan from before time itself.

Consequently, her justification had precedence over her works. Her works simply confirmed that her faith was real. Again, James used the word *justify* to mean prove. Her works proved or revealed her faith. And, consistent with God's method of salvation, Rahab's faith was justified by the free grace of God. Rahab wasn't saved because she did what she did. Rather, she did what she did because she was saved by the free grace of God—and she knew it.

James used examples that inverted the temporal sequence of works and salvation in order to establish that the relationship between them is not dependent upon time. Abraham was saved (justified) long before he offered to sacrifice Isaac. And Rahab worked a deal (saved the spies) long before she was saved (from the siege).

The two examples taken together, then, cannot be understood to explain faith and works in a temporal way. The relationship between them is not sequential, as if human works must come before God's justification. Rather, the relationship between them stands outside of time. It is what we might call a logical relationship, though the logic is God's, not ours. The only conclusion that can be drawn from James' examples is that God's justification is always by means of His free grace, and that it always requires confirmation by bearing the fruit of the Spirit.

In a sense, both the credit and the debit sides of the ledger require the correct entry to make the divine transaction complete. An entry is made on the credit side as God accounts Christ's righteousness to the church—her members individually and collectively. But an entry must also be made as people debit Christ's righteousness for themselves.

SUMMING UP

James sums up chapter two: "For as the body without the spirit is dead, so faith without works is dead also" (v. 26). Works are animated by faith in the same way that the body is animated by the spirit. The body is the vehicle of the spirit, as works provide the vehicle for faith. A dead body is a body without a spirit, so dead faith is faith without fruit.

Christ died for the atonement of sin, to reconcile all of His people to God. Salvation requires that people know that the Messiah has saved them from their sins. Yet at the same time, knowing that the Messiah died to save sinners is no guarantee of salvation. Even the demons know that Christ died to save sinners. Saved sinners always know that Christ died for them personally.

While it is true that God loves sinners just as they are, He doesn't want them to remain just as they are—sinners. Many people reject God's love and remain in sin. Consequently, the fact that God's love is unconditional does not mean that everyone will be saved. Rather, it means that God doesn't save people on account of any conditions they might fulfill. However, the fact that salvation is unconditional does not mean that there are not certain character manifestations that are produced by salvation, certain fruits of the spirit.

Has your name been written in the "Lamb's Book of Life?" (Revelation 21:27). Have you been to the bank of God's salvation and drawn on your line of credit? Have you cashed your check? Have you debited the righteousness of Christ?

Caution: Steep Grade

My brethren, let not many of you become teachers, knowing that we
shall receive a stricter judgment. For we all stumble in many things.
If anyone does not stumble in word, he is a perfect man, able also to
bridle the whole body. Indeed, we put bits in horses' mouths that they
may obey us, and we turn their whole body. Look also at ships:
although they are so large and are driven by fierce winds, they are
turned by a very small rudder wherever the pilot desires. Even so the
tongue is a little member and boasts great things. See how great a
forest a little fire kindles! —James 3:1-5

James opens chapter three with a caution about teaching the Bible to others. This is not likely what Christian Education Committees want to hear. I can hear people thinking, "How can he preach such a verse when we are in need of Sunday School teachers? Wouldn't it be better to encourage potential teachers to step forward in confidence than to discourage them with warnings about greater responsibilities?" Be that as it may, we are faced here with the reality of the awesome responsibility of biblical leadership. The Bible simply presents the facts as they actually are.

James warns all would-be teachers that God will judge them more strictly than He will judge others. Teachers must be, not only confident enough, but right enough in their understanding of the Bible that they are willing to submit themselves to a higher standard. So much for equality before the Lord! Indeed, James explicitly says here that all are not equal before God, but that the bar is higher for teachers, and by implication, for other church leaders. Paul's letters to Timothy and Titus confirm that all church leaders (elders and deacons) must also be experienced in teaching. They must be "teachable" (1 Timothy 3:2), that is, they must be both able to be taught and able to teach others.

There are at least two benefits that come from leaders who have come up through the ranks of the local church. First, their knowledge of Scripture and doctrine will be known and accepted by the members. Such knowledge will provide both assurance and ability to their various responsibilities within the church. Secondly, because of the exposure they give of themselves through the office of teaching, and because of the opportunities teachers have to conform their own beliefs and values to Scripture, the more unified the leadership will be. It is hard for teachers to hide what they believe. Thus, such local church educated leaders will engender greater trust among the people, and greater ability in their leadership functions.

James recommends a win-win situation. Everyone wins when the qualifications for teachers and leaders are set at the scriptural mark. Yet, it must be understood that the Lord does not require teachers to know everything, just to be teachable themselves. James says that the reason that teachers must be graded by a higher standard is that "we all stumble in many things" (v. 2). Because we are all prone to stumble, we don't need leaders who will help us stumble even more. We need leaders who will help us not to stumble. We can stumble perfectly well over ourselves. Our own feet trip us up often enough. We don't need to stumble over our leaders as well. If anything, church leaders should keep people from stumbling, not cause them to stumble. The best defense against such stumbling, says James, is not leadership ability, but knowledge of Scripture—knowing enough to teach. Thus, Scripture sets a higher mark.

THE GIFT OF GAB

Leadership ability is often associated with the gift of gab, a function of the tongue. Hence, James' caution. James said that those who can keep their tongues from erring, will be able to keep their bodies and behavior from error as well. Why? Because the tongue is like a rudder to the body. Where the tongue leads, so goes the whole person.

It is an interesting thought that we can steer the course of our lives with our tongues. James uses the analogy of a ship where the rudder guides the ship. We can add that the pilot steers the rudder according to the orders of the captain. The human mind is the pilot and Christ is the captain—unless, of course, Satan is sitting in the captain's seat, or the pilot is steering his own course. But in the church and among Christians, Christ ought to be captain.

When Christ gives the orders and the pilot is trustworthy, the ship will be bound for glory. But whenever the chain of command breaks down—be it that Satan countermands the orders, or the pilot fails to steer as directed, or the rudder does not correctly respond to the wheel —the ship goes off course.

James' point is that the pilot, the one who steers the ship, has a greater responsibility for arriving at the destination than does, say, the cook, or whoever. The pilot is not to steer as he thinks best. He is not free to go wherever he wants to go. Rather, he is to abide by the orders of the captain.

Not everyone can be a good pilot. It would be disastrous to allow the entire crew to randomly rotate into the position of pilot. On the other hand, it is most useful to train those who show interest and aptitude. Does that mean that the pilot is "better" than the rest of the crew? As undemocratic as it sounds, the answer really is *yes*. He's better at piloting.

Certainly, you wouldn't want any old yahoo at the helm. There are certain abilities and qualifications that are necessary for the job, and not everyone is able to meet them. The pilot must have a certain amount of training and experience. Training and experience are necessary for most any job, some more than others. Certainly the pilot should be better at piloting than others.

I can look at an x-ray, but I don't see what a qualified and experienced doctor will see. He will see things that are meaningless to me. What he has been trained to see is critical to his job—and to the health of his patients. The doctor may show me what he sees, and I may see it and I may not. He may explain it to me and I may understand it and I may not. But in the long run I must trust his judgment above my own because of his training and experience.

I can listen to the engine of my car, but I don't hear what a qualified and experienced mechanic hears. He hears things that are meaningless to me. What he has been trained to hear is critical to his job. He may point it out to me and I may hear it and I may not. He may explain it to me and I may or may not understand it. But in the long run I will yield to his opinion because of his training and experience—or go else-where. To do otherwise is foolish.

One would think that the same thing is true in the church, except that in the contemporary church people think themselves to be experts. "Preachers and teachers are no better than anyone else," they say. "What makes their opinion any better than mine?" Indeed, that is the crux of the issue. Why should we listen to preachers and teachers? What is the role of church leaders?

In our lust for egalitarianism (equality among all before God) we have mistaken the fact that God loves all of His children with the falsity that all of His beloved children are equally endowed with obedience, understanding, and ability. I believe that the crisis of leadership that presently confronts the contemporary church is a direct result of this mistaken belief. Churches are too ready to grant leadership to anyone who wants it, and too hesitant to maintain the biblical qualifications of leadership. The result is a lack of respect and trust of church leaders on the part of church members that results in a lack of obedience.

Those who are drawn into a deeper relationship with the Lord—often leaders, but not always—are sometimes accused of thinking that they are better than others. While most church leaders do not think that, no Christian would deny the superior value of growing and maturing in biblical terms and biblical understanding. If knowledge of the Lord is good, then more knowledge is better. Yet, salvation is not a matter of knowledge, but of God's grace. The issue here is not knowledge as a way of attaining salvation, but of the role of knowledge in the ongoing sanctification of the redeemed, and its basis for church leadership.

The Lord's ways are not like our ways. Those who are called to a deeper relationship with the Lord are not elevated above others in order to lord it over them. Rather, leaders themselves should be brought to their knees in humility before the Lord as they grow in grace. Humility is the doorway to a deeper relationship with God. It is the eye of the needle that the self-sufficient will not pass through. It is the one thing needful of young, wealthy movers and shakers. It is the pearl of great price. It is the practical application of Scripture. It is the stumbling block of many.

A genuine relationship with God does not bring anyone to the pinnacle of the temple in glory, but to the foot of the cross in humility.

Those on their way to the pinnacle of the temple ought not be followed, for they will be the downfall of many. Rather, at the last day God will raise on high those He finds laboring at the foot of the cross.

THE HIGHER STANDARD OF HUMILITY

What a paradox! The higher standard expected of teachers and leaders does not lead upward in glory, but downward in humility. Rather, the height of the gospel standard points to a steep and dangerous downgrade that leads to the foot of the cross. Many Christian leaders and teachers, hoping to soar to the heights of glory, find that the road suddenly drops from their sight as it plummets to the floor of the valley of the shadow of death.

Caution, says James, steep grade ahead. Fasten your seat belts, guard your tongues, and trust the Lord.

THESE THINGS OUGHT NOT TO BE SO

And the tongue is a fire, a world of iniquity. The tongue is so set among our members that it defiles the whole body, and sets on fire the course of nature; and it is set on fire by hell. For every kind of beast and bird, of reptile and creature of the sea, is tamed and has been tamed by mankind. But no man can tame the tongue. It is an unruly evil, full of deadly poison. With it we bless our God and Father, and with it we curse men, who have been made in the similitude of God. Out of the same mouth proceed blessing and cursing. My brethren, these things ought not to be so. Does a spring send forth fresh water and bitter from the same opening? Can a fig tree, my brethren, bear olives, or a grapevine bear figs? Thus no spring yields both salt water and fresh. —James 3:6-12

The club was celebrating its 10th anniversary with a formal dinner catered in their meeting hall. Finally all the guests had arrived and were seated when the emcee made all the necessary announcements and called upon the local pastor to pray the blessing.

The pastor waxed eloquent, citing in his prayer the great accomplishments of the club, the wonder, grace, and mercy of God, thankfulness for all things—especially for the blessings God had given through the many works of the club in the neighborhood, and finally extolling the virtues of always speaking kindness and encouragement. Amen.

The head table was served before the quiet of the prayer had elapsed. As the pastor sat down at his place, he no more looked at his plate only to see a sickly colored and slightly crusted beef stroganoff, turned to his wife and exclaimed loud enough for all to hear, "What kind of garbage is this?" The hall exploded in laughter, noting the incongruity of the human tongue.

Four Points

James established that the tongue is powerful, and that its power can be for good or evil. He then offered four points to support his proposition. First, he said that the tongue has the power to control our lives (v. 3-5). Second, he pointed to the destructive power of the tongue (v. 5-6). Third, he indicated the inability of man to control the tongue (v. 7-10). 4) And lastly, he said that these things ought not to be (v. 10-12).

It has been said that the eyes are the window of the soul. It ought also to be said that the tongue is the megaphone of the heart. Jesus said that "those things which proceed out of the mouth come from the heart, and they defile a man" (Matthew 15:18). Words originate in the thoughts and values of people. Selfish thoughts and Godless values are the springboard of selfish and Godless words.

Human speech accurately reveals human character, said Jesus. It was not the Pharisee's actions or forms of worship that troubled the Lord, it was their unrepentant character that continued to find fault in Jesus' ministry. At every point the hardhearted Pharisees had failed to see Jesus' miracles, or the wonder of God's grace, mercy, and patience.

James flatly says that the tongue is a world of iniquity and unrighteousness. If the tongue were consistently iniquitous there would be no problem believing that people are totally depraved, that sin dominates human consciousness, that people are completely unable to correct their own faults.

When James said that every wild animal can be tamed, but the tongue cannot, he didn't mean the simple restraining of our words, but bringing our deepest thoughts and values into conformity with God's will. For the tongue gives wings to our thoughts and values. James' insinuation leads directly to the sinful condition of the hearts of all men. The human tongue is the best weapon that Satan has.

But lest we think that the taming of wild beasts originates in the skills and abilities of men, we need to be reminded that God gave Adam dominion over the creatures of the world (Genesis 1:26-28), and that dominion was renewed after the Flood (Genesis 9:1-7). We have dominion over animals because God has given it. All human skills and abilities are gifts from God. We have no reason to boast of human power, creativity, or ingenuity.

Consequently, the untamable nature of the tongue should point us all to our desperate need for a Savior. The problem is deeper than the fact that we badmouth each other and God all too often. The problem of the tongue points to the problem of the heart, the problem of human sin and of our unwillingness to submit to the authority of the Savior, or His Word—or to honor any authority except our own.

TAMING THE TONGUE

To tame the tongue—or any animal—it must become subject to another. Domesticated or tame animals have given up their right to exercise their own will. They are not their own master, or the captain of their own ship. Rather, they stand in submission to the will of another master. That is what it means to tame an animal.

Similarly, the civilizing of man requires the domestication of his will. So Christ stands at the apex of civilization as the Master of all. Ultimately, there can be no civil society, no civil authority without submission to Christ. God insists that humanity learn this lesson one way or the other. As submission to Christ has waned in the twentieth century, so the foundations of civil authority and society have crumbled in its wake.

And just as civilized men must serve one another in Christ, they must also be in submission first to Christ Himself, and then to one another in Christ. Jesus said, "Assuredly, I say to you, inasmuch as you did it to one of the least of these My brethren, you did it to Me." (Matthew 25:40). As service is rendered to the least, it is rendered to Christ. And as submission is rendered to Christ, it is rendered to the least of His representatives. If you are looking for Christ you can find Him in service to the least of the brethren. People look far and wide to find Christ, but fail to stoop to the place where He is always found—in humble service.

It would be difficult to find a more convicting verse of Scripture than this passage in James. James strikes with deadly accuracy at the inconsistencies of human character. The picture he painted is not pretty, but it is accurate. And in this it has value. The same mouth blesses and curses. The same mouth encourages and condemns. The same mouth kisses and bites. The point that James drives home is that a double tongue reveals a double mind.

Such double-mindedness is not new or unique in our time. It has been a consistent and recurring problem among God's people. What are we to think when people—even Christians—say one thing and do another? What are we to think when we encounter divided words, divided loyalties, divided commitments?

The answer is not difficult to understand. Yet it is difficult to assimilate because we so often find ourselves stumbling because of our own divided words, divided loyalties, and divided commitments. To identify the problem accurately is to accuse ourselves of what is unspeakable in God's church. How can God's church, the community of the redeemed be so full of so many unsaved sinners?

James said it, not me. I'm only applying God's Word to our situation. James said that a bitter tongue accurately represents a bitter spirit. Such a spirit is not of God, for God is not bitter, but sweet.

The fact that "no spring yields both salt water and fresh" (v. 12) alludes to the fact that there is no third or neutral position regarding salvation. People are either saved or lost. There is no middle ground.

Thus, when gossiping, back-biting, complaining and the like erupt in the church, it is evidence that the purity of the church has been compromised. None of this is, of course, new to us. We have known for centuries that the church is a compromised institution, though God promises that it will one day be pure. Jesus acknowledged that the wheat and the tares grow together in the world "until the time of harvest" (Matthew 13:30, 38). The power of James' point, then, is directed at individual Christians who comprise the church. Each individual is called to purity.

SHAPE UP OR SHIP OUT

The most effective remedy for a church that is plagued with such problems is found in the lives of individual believers. The church as a whole can do little to correct the problem. But individual Christians must apply these verses to themselves. Some tongue waggers will grow in grace by the power of the Holy Spirit and modify their behavior to please the Lord. Others who thought they were Christian, but find that they have no interest in curbing their tongues or pleasing the Lord, will discover that they are not. The second group should leave the church.

While on one hand this may sound harsh and cruel, it is not. It is no more cruel than submitting to surgery. While there is pain involved, the procedure produces the best for the body in the long run. Real Christians need to face their inconsistencies and bring their lives into conformity with Scripture—and the sooner the better. False Christians—people who misunderstand the gospel and align themselves with a church for the wrong reasons—need to face the fact of their misunderstanding, and either 1) bring their lives into conformity with Scripture, or 2) quit pretending to be Christian by virtue of their church association. The more unpleasant alternative is for the church to take disciplinary action. This remedy is not the product of the minds of men, but of the mind of God (Matthew 18:15-17).

Lord, have mercy!

WISDOM FROM ABOVE

Can a fig tree, my brethren, bear olives, or a grapevine bear figs?
Thus no spring yields both salt water and fresh. Who is wise and
understanding among you? Let him show by good conduct that his
works are done in the meekness of wisdom. But if you have bitter
envy and self-seeking in your hearts, do not boast and lie against the
truth. This wisdom does not descend from above, but is earthly,
sensual, demonic. For where envy and self-seeking exist, confusion
and every evil thing are there. But the wisdom that is from above is
first pure, then peaceable, gentle, willing to yield, full of mercy and
good fruits, without partiality and without hypocrisy. Now the fruit
of righteousness is sown in peace by those who make peace.
—James 3:12-18

James here contrasts the ways of the godly and the ways of the
ungodly. The ungodly are characterized with words like, bitter envy,
self-seeking, boasting, lying, earthliness, sensuality, and hypocrisy.
Godliness, on the other hand, is characterized by "the meekness of
wisdom," which is "pure, peaceable, gentle, willing to yield, full of
mercy and good fruits, without partiality and without hypocrisy" (v.
17). Pointing to the application of biblical principles, James contrasts the
fruit of godliness with the fruit of ungodliness.

Donald Barnhouse tells the story of a young immigrant who had
been brought up in the slums of New York City, who rose to fame,
stardom, and wealth. He bought a yacht and hired a man to run it for
him, but he took the title of "captain" for himself. He had a tailor make
him a beautiful captain's uniform, complete with gold braid, brass but-
tons, and captain's hat.

He wanted to impress his mother, who had grown up in the Old Country. So, one day he put on his captain's uniform, and took his aging mother out into the bay. Standing proudly on the yacht, with the wind in his face and his mother next to him, he said, "Look mamma, I'm a captain."

His mother, nearly two heads shorter than he, gnarled and bent with age, hosting the wisdom of the Old Country in her eyes, replied, "By you, you is a captain, and by me, you is a captain. But by captains you ain't no captain."

We can apply this old saint's wisdom more generally. The saintly mother would say to the world, "By our own measure we are doing pretty well, and by the measure of our neighbors or society we are good people—perhaps among the best. But by God's measure we have no goodness at all." Isaiah said, "We are all like an unclean thing, And all our righteousnesses are like filthy rags" (Isaiah 64:6). The measure used always makes a great deal of difference.

James' primary insight here is that godly wisdom is characterized by humility and meekness. "The meek shall inherit the earth, And shall delight themselves in the abundance of peace" (Psalms 37:11), writes the Psalmist. Similarly, Jesus said, "Blessed are the meek, For they shall inherit the earth" (Matthew 5:5). God's people are to be meek people. But what is meekness?

The Power Of The Meek

The dictionary says that the "meek" are patient and mild, not inclined to anger or resentment. That seems to be what Scripture means as well. But the dictionary goes on to add variations of meaning, i.e., "easily imposed on, spineless, spiritless." Jesus is the model Christian, and Jesus was anything but spineless or spiritless. In fact, these definitions are actually the very opposite of real meekness. To be meek is not to be weak, but to be obedient, and there is no correlation between obedience and weakness. So, these dictionary definitions reflect worldly attitudes and are clearly not what Scripture means.

But was Jesus easily imposed on? Jesus did a lot of things for a lot of people. Did they impose themselves upon Jesus?

Matthew tells a story about Jesus that may help us. One day "a ruler came and worshiped Him, saying, 'My daughter has just died, but come and lay Your hand on her and she will live.' So Jesus arose and followed him..." (Matthew 9:18-19). Did this ruler impose upon Jesus? Well, in a way he did. But Jesus did not consider it an imposition.

An imposition is laid upon someone when he is coerced into doing something that he wouldn't otherwise do. But Jesus wanted to do God's will, so He went willingly. He was not coerced. The Scriptures are filled with these kinds of stories. People were always coming to Jesus and asking for this or that, for healing, salvation, or miracles of various kinds. And Jesus often performed as He was asked. But not always.

When Mary imposed upon Jesus to turn water into wine at the wedding at Cana, Jesus complied. Clearly, this miracle of Jesus' was given as a sign of his divinity. But later,

> "some of the scribes and Pharisees (said), 'Teacher, we want to see a sign from You.' But He answered and said to them, 'An evil and adulterous generation seeks after a sign, and no sign will be given to it except the sign of the prophet Jonah'" (Matthew 12:38-39).

He would not be imposed upon by them. So, what was the difference? Both wanted a sign. Both requested some action from Jesus.

The difference was who is doing the imposing and the end or purpose for which they were doing it. Again, an imposition is a coercion that goes against one's natural tendency. The difference was that the miracle at Cana agreed with God's will, and the request of the Pharisees did not.

Jesus was meek. He was patient and mild, not inclined to anger or resentment. Yet, Jesus was also capable of anger. One day He was teaching in the Temple when the Pharisees began to accost Him about His gospel. He saw a man with a withered hand and called him forward.

> "And when He had looked around at them *with anger*, being grieved by the hardness of their hearts, He said to the man, 'Stretch out your hand.' And he stretched it out, and his hand was restored as whole as the other" (Mark 3:5—italics added).

Jesus was also angry when He overturned the tables of the money changers. The point is that anger and boldness are not incompatible with meekness.

It has been said that a fine race horse will have the quality of meek-ness. The horse will be tame, yet strong and bold when required. A meek race horse is readily responsive to the commands of the jockey. The jockey does not have to fight with the horse. Meekness here means responsive to guidance.

THE WISDOM OF THE MEEK

Jesus was meek, but not regarding the frivolous desires of men. Rather, He was meek to God's guidance. He had a discriminating meekness. And so must we. Jesus was responsive to the wisdom from above, God's wisdom, the wisdom of Scripture.

James provides the defining characteristics of God's wisdom. He said that

> "the wisdom that is from above is first pure, then peaceable,
> gentle, willing to yield, full of mercy and good fruits, without
> partiality and without hypocrisy" (v. 17).

Meekness shares many of the characteristics of the fruits of the spirit. It is pure, peaceful, gentle, obedient, merciful, and full of "love, joy, peace, long-suffering, kindness, goodness, faithfulness, gentleness, (and) self-control" (Galatians 5:22-23).

It is instructive to notice that James' definition of wisdom is not intellectual. James didn't include *smart* in his list. Nor did Paul. God's wisdom is not a matter of intellectual ability or education or IQ or any other measure associated with human ability. God's wisdom is com-pletely different from what people naturally associate with human wis-dom. In fact, all of James' characteristics of wisdom are behavioral. They are actions and attitudes. And as such they are available to every-one. They do not belong to a special class of people who are endowed with special abilities or advantages. Such is God's grace!

PURE

God's wisdom is pure. The Greek word for pure is *hagnos*, and means innocent, modest, chaste, clean. To be innocent is to be free from sin, evil, and guilt. No wonder God's wisdom is "from above." It couldn't possibly be from man. Men are sinful, depraved, and guilty. Anything that comes from the human heart or mind must, therefore, be contaminated with these things.

Can innocence and purity be recovered when they have once been lost? Trying to recover innocence is like trying to recover virginity. It really cannot be done. And yet an interesting thing is happening in the world of Christian sex education. Christians are being taught that through the forgiveness of Christ people can recover a kind of secondary virginity. Because in Christ all things are renewed, there is a sense in which virginity can be restored. Scripture says that "the blood of Jesus Christ his Son cleanses us from all sin" (1 John 1:17), not *some* sin, but *all* sin. In fact, God's forgiveness works on all sin in the same way. Sin is cleansed away. It is removed and the previous condition is restored. Praise the Lord!

PEACEABLE

James tells us that God's wisdom is peaceable (*eirenikos*). The Greek word means the opposite of a state of war. Peace among men begins in peace with God. The Hebrew word is *shalom*. The peace or *shalom* of the New Testament is the awaited eschatological (or end time) salvation. It is the purpose for which "the whole creation groans and labors with birth pangs" (Romans 8:22). Paul cried out, Lord, free us from the crisis of labor and travail! The church—and the whole world—is writhing in labor for the second birth. It was when Paul wrote, and it still is today. What can we do to bear it? We must grit our teeth and bear down upon it. We must brace ourselves for the agony of every contraction, in the hope of the delivery to come. Come, Lord Jesus!

GENTLE

James tells us that God's wisdom is gentle. The Greek word is *epieikes*, and means appropriate. By implication God's wisdom is mild and gentle. It is appropriate because it is fitting. God's wisdom fits the need. It is not forced because it is a product of God's grace. Like the gentle dripping of water in a cave that over time can create a stalactite or a stalagmite. God's wisdom is gentle as it moves unswervingly and unfailingly toward its end.

WILLING TO YIELD

God's wisdom is willing to yield, the Greek *eupeithes*, means easily persuaded. Wisdom wants to do what it right, and always yields to righteousness. Christians yield to what is right according to God's standard, regardless of who speaks it. By God's wisdom Christians do not come kicking and screaming into the Kingdom. They are easily persuaded of Christ's truth and righteousness. It is only when people try to come to Christ by their own resources that they kick and scream and resist the Spirit. But God's wisdom is persevering and will abide to the end because God's plan cannot fail.

Full Of Mercy

God's wisdom is full of mercy—*eleos*—compassion and tender mercy. We can be thankful that God's wisdom includes mercy. If it didn't, we wouldn't be here. We would be casualties of God's wrath. But God's wisdom is merciful because God is merciful.

Impartial

God's wisdom is also impartial—*adiakritos*. This Greek word has many meanings—indistinguishable, imprecise, obscure, impartial, without distinction. It has the sense of being unbiased, just, and fair regarding judgment. While we often feel compelled to make excuses for the faithlessness of our families and friends, our children and parents, God's judgment is impartial. God's judgment is always true and right and fair. God never misjudges anything.

Without Hypocrisy

Finally, then, God's wisdom is without hypocrisy—*anupokritos*, without pretense, misrepresentation, or fraud. It is what it appears to be. It does not "get along to go along," but speaks its mind in love. It does not posture and play politics for the sake of some compromised gain. It is what it is, come what may. It does not compromise, but holds forth the truth. But God's wisdom can afford to be that way because it is always right.

We, too, must be without hypocrisy. But, unlike God, we are not always right. Therefore, we must rely on God's wisdom, and the only place to find God's wisdom is in Scripture. No wonder evangelical Christians think so highly of God's Book. Our very lives hang in its balance.

When we are not right, which is all of the time when we are not genuinely led by the Holy Spirit in the light of Scripture, we must repent of our errors. Sometimes we are wrong even when we think we are right about Scripture. Thus, we must be willing to admit to our own errors, but insist that the correction be biblical. We don't need to dwell on our errors. We don't need to recount them. We don't need to repeat them. But we do need to repent of them.

To repent is to change our mind, to come into agreement with God. But if we just feel bad and change our minds without also changing our behavior, we have not really repented. For repentance also requires a change of behavior. We need to consult Scripture and be obedient to it. We must conform our behavior to Scripture. That is repentance.

Christians can do that because Christ died on the cross in order to free them from the curse of making their own mistakes over and over again. He gave His life in order to break the cycle of sin and death that so captivates the whole world. His death on the cross has provided a new opportunity for humanity. Even now in our postmodern world. Even in the midst of the sin and sorrow in which we find ourselves. A new opportunity in Christ is ours for the repenting.

He died for you, won't you repent for Him? What an opportunity we have! Won't you take it to the Lord in prayer.

You Ask Amiss

Where do wars and fights come from among you? Do they not come from your desires for pleasure that war in your members? You lust and do not have. You murder and covet and cannot obtain. You fight and war. Yet you do not have because you do not ask. You ask and do not receive, because you ask amiss, that you may spend it on your pleasures. Adulterers and adulteresses! Do you not know that friendship with the world is enmity with God? Whoever therefore wants to be a friend of the world makes himself an enemy of God. Or do you think that the Scripture says in vain, "The Spirit who dwells in us yearns jealously"? But He gives more grace. Therefore He says: "God resists the proud, But gives grace to the humble." Therefore submit to God. Resist the devil and he will flee from you. Draw near to God and He will draw near to you. Cleanse your hands, you sinners; and purify your hearts, you double-minded. Lament and mourn and weep! Let your laughter be turned to mourning and your joy to gloom. Humble yourselves in the sight of the Lord, and He will lift you up. —James 4:1-10

There is an old fable about the wolves and the dogs. It seems that at one time wolves were afraid of dogs because there were so many more of them and they were so well fed and strong. One day the wolves sent a scout to learn what he could by watching the dogs. The wolf scout returned to the pack and reported.

"It is true that they are many and well fed," he said. "But there are not many who can harm us. There are a lot of different kinds of dogs—big, little, long hair, short hair, floppy ears, pointed ears, long snouts, flat snouts, etc. But as I watched them I noticed that they were all snapping at each other. I saw that, while they hate us wolves, they hate each other even more. They will not bother us."

The fable could be a story about the church. Paul said,

> "For all the law is fulfilled in one word, even in this: 'You shall love your neighbor as yourself.' But if you bite and devour one another, beware lest you be consumed by one another!" (Galatians 5:14-15).

As long as the church is consumed with internal bickering and infighting, Satan has nothing to worry about. The church will not bother him.

In chapter four James considered the origin, nature, and resolution of human conflict. There are many people who don't want to concern themselves with the negativity of the origins and nature of human conflict. Fortunately, James isn't one of them. He meets the problem head on, as must we if we are to be biblical in our treatment of it.

James begins with the origin of wars and fights. His concern is not merely armed combat, but the thoughts and feelings that lead to war. He identifies the desire for pleasure—having what I want, having things my way—as the primary culprit. His use of the word *murder* is consistent with his war analogy, but again he identifies envy and covetousness as the passions that give rise to strife and ultimately armed combat.

In three verses James has laid out the origins of human conflict— selfishness, envy, and covetousness. This list can be further distilled. Envy is wanting what someone else has, covetousness is wanting what you don't have, and the desire for pleasure is just plain wanting. It all boils down to selfishness. When people have to have things *their* way, the inevitable result is strife, dissension, conflict, and struggle, which in turn often lead to war and murder. All this comes from the single root of selfishness.

BUT DADDY

At dinner one of the children had a question about what she ought to do regarding a particular incident that happened at school. After dinner the child followed the father out of the dining room into the study. The father repeated the answer he had given at the dinner table.

"But Daddy..." the child insisted, and tried a different approach to the matter.

Mother overheard the new approach and came in to see what response her husband would make. As the mother entered the room, the child turned to her and whined, "I'm trying to find out what Daddy wants me to do."

At that point the father interrupted, "No you're not. You're not trying to find out what I want you to do. You're trying to see if you can get me to change the conditions I set so that you can do what you want, instead of doing what I want. Now, go and do as you are told!"

Don't we all argue this way with God and with one another.

James said, "You do not have because you do not ask" (v. 3). Just as the child wasn't really asking her father, we try to get God to give us what *we* want rather than what *He* wants us to have. She wasn't asking her father, she was telling him what she wanted and what she thought he should do about it. So many prayers are like that! We tell God what we want and what He should do about it.

"You ask and you don't receive," James continued, "because you ask amiss that you may spend it on your pleasures" (v. 3). James echoed a theme that runs throughout Scripture—God doesn't always answer prayer. Does Scripture really teach that God doesn't always answer prayer?

> Job 35:12, "There they cry out, but He does not answer, because of the pride of evil men."
>
> Psalm 18:41, "They cried out, but there was none to save; even to the Lord, but He did not answer them."
>
> Proverbs 1:28, "Then they will call on me, but I will not answer; they will seek me diligently, but they will not find me."
>
> Isaiah 1:15, "When you spread out your hands, I will hide My eyes from you; even though you make many prayers, I will not hear. Your hands are full of blood."
>
> Jeremiah 11:14, "So do not pray for this people, or lift up a cry or prayer for them; for I will not hear them in the time that they cry out to Me because of their trouble."
>
> Jeremiah 14:12, "When they fast, I will not hear their cry; and when they offer burnt offering and grain offering, I will not

accept them. But I will consume them by the sword, by the
famine, and by the pestilence."

Micah 3:4, "Then they will cry to the Lord, But He will not hear
them; He will even hide His face from them at that time, because
they have been evil in their deeds."

James may have been thinking about these verses as he told the
church that God was not going to answer their selfish prayers. While it
is true that Jesus said, "whatever you ask the Father in My name He will
give you" (John 16:23). It is also true that "he who says, 'I know Him,'
and does not keep His commandments, is a liar, and the truth is not in
him" (1 John 2:4). The secret of getting what you want from God is
wanting what He wants you to have.

James realized the seriousness of their situation, that God may not
answer them, but give them up to "uncleanness, in the lusts of their
hearts," as Paul said in Romans 1:24. It is not beyond God to chastise
His people, nor to permit them to suffer the consequences of their own
folly. In fact, it is one of God's regular practices.

James lost all sense of propriety at this point. He accused them all of
adultery. They all were guilty—men and women alike, not just the
heads of the households, nor just the heads of the church, but everyone.
The allusion to adultery is another common theme in Scripture. God
claims the privilege of marriage rights with His people. He is the husband, the church is His bride. She is to be in submission to Him. And
following the marriage allusions, the primary way in which God relates
to His people is by His covenant.

By that covenant He purchased the church for His own (Psalm
74:2, Acts 20:28). We are His sheep, He is our Shepherd. The relationship between the Lord and His people is covenantal, just like marriage.
Any abuse of that covenant amounts to an act of adultery, according to
Scripture. Long before adultery breaks out into sexual indiscretion,
there are abuses of the promises and responsibilities of the covenant.

Adultery so often begins with a supposedly "harmless" friendship
with someone at the office, a neighbor across the street, a listening ear,
a sympathetic heart. The friendship grows by insinuation and innuendo, flirting and fascination. A tone of voice becomes a touch, a touch
becomes a hug. What began benignly, grows with interest and attention, and soon blossoms into the poison flower of sin.

Similarly, James said that "friendship with the world is enmity with God" (v. 4). Friendship with the world leads to spiritual laxity, and spiritual laxity to infidelity to God's covenant, and adultery. If there is a root problem in the contemporary church it is surely worldliness. Contemporary Christianity is so worldly that Christians of bygone years would hardly recognize it as Christianity at all! Americans are no longer products of fidelity to God's covenant, if indeed they ever truly were.

The contemporary age is the product of the most thorough-going campaign of worldliness that the world has ever seen. We are all breaded and deep-fried in the saturated fat of modern commercialism. Commercialism is the spirit of doing things primarily for financial gain. It is the intrusion of economic values into every aspect of life and living. It is always watching out for the bottom line. When the bottom line becomes the top priority, commercialism reigns king.

I don't mean that we should cast three sheets to the wind and disregard financial responsibility. But I am saying that there are some things in life that are more important than their effect on our pocketbook. Faith often puts finances at odds with God's will. Jesus didn't tell the disciples to go and make disciples of all the nations as soon as they thought they could afford it (Matthew 28:19). He didn't send them to build His church when or as they could make time for it. No one can afford to do what God calls them to do! But God calls them to do it anyway because He will provide.

It is also true that Jesus told his disciples to count the cost of their projects before they began them (Luke 14:28). He didn't want them to fail to finish what they began. But he didn't mean that the project shouldn't be done if they couldn't afford it. Rather, they were to count the cost so that they would know how much money and material they needed to raise. The point of the story is proper preparation. It is not to serve as an excuse for doing nothing! Count the cost, make the necessary preparations, get what you need to do it all, and then, by all means, do it!

DRAW NEAR

It has been said that pride is the greatest sin and the root of all the others. Pride is self-centeredness, which is nothing more than selfishness. James says that "God resists the proud" (v. 6). Nothing will keep

God away like pride and selfishness. In any situation the blessings of God can be quickly dispersed by the expression of pride and selfishness.

"But," says James, God "gives grace to the humble" (v. 6). So, just as God can be kept away through pride and selfishness, so God can be coaxed near with humility and selflessness. Humility "suffers long and is kind; (it) does not envy; (it) does not parade itself, is not puffed up; does not behave rudely, does not seek its own, is not provoked, thinks no evil; does not rejoice in iniquity, but rejoices in the truth; bears all things, believes all things, hopes all things, endures all things" (1 Corinthians 13:4-7). Humility never fails. There is only one road to humility. It is the road of submission to Christ, submission to the Word of God, submission to the ways of God.

James provides one of the most important verses in Scripture, "Draw near to God and He will draw near to you" (v. 7). James is not talking about works-righteousness, as if we can cause God to bless us. We cannot cause God to do anything. He is a free agent. Yet, as we draw near to God in humility, He will reciprocate because He chooses to do so and promised that He always will.

Do you have any idea of the potential advantage that this knowledge contains? Everything hinges on being in right relationship with God. We are invited to "draw near to God" and given the promise that by so doing "He will draw near" (v. 8) to us. But how shall we draw near? How shall we approach the throne of the Almighty?

James told us, "cleanse your hands...purify your hearts.... Lament and mourn and weep...humble yourselves" (vs. 8-10). The first of these further instructions—cleansing and purifying—are in part a matter of cleaning up our act. Note that James was talking to church members. The suggestion that church members needed to be cleansed and purified meant that they were dirty and impure. James acknowledged that the Christians he wrote to needed such purification, and by implication so do we. It means that we must come to the realization that we are not only guilty of doing the wrong things, but we are guilty of having the wrong motives. Both our actions and our motives are wrong. We are a fallen and sinful people living in a fallen and sinful world.

We all must not only change what we have been doing, but we must change the way we have been doing it and the purpose for which we have been doing it. James spoke to people in the church of his day, and his lessons still apply. The Holy Spirit has spoken these words to the whole world, and more specifically to His church. Prayers go unanswered. We have asked amiss because we all seek our own pleasure. Christians today are self-centered, self-possessed, and self-deluded. But it is not the first time in history that this has been the case.

God's reply is to insist that repentance come before renewal. But in order to repent, Christians must understand that they are in the wrong. We are worldly and selfish to a person. We are "double minded" (v. 8), divided, and broken. I am not just being negative. I am not depressed and without hope. Rather, it is the recognition of our brokenness and failure that offers our only real hope. The recognition of Christian brokenness and failure is not negative, but actually provides an opportunity for the healing love of Christ by the grace of God to fall upon the church. But we must realize that God's healing begins with the recognition and confession of brokenness. There can be no healing apart from such recognition and confession.

We all want God's healing, don't we? But we don't want to feel our brokenness. So, we jump to conclusions by supplying our own answers. We don't have the patience to wait upon the Lord, so we try to beat God by jumping to our own conclusions. People supply their own answers to their own problems. With so many available answers there shouldn't be any problems. But there are! Our problems remain in spite of the spate of so-called Christian answers offered in the Christian book stores.

We must listen to the Lord, not to ourselves. The preacher's responsibility is to make God's Word clear, but no one wants to hear it. The truth is that people have failed to obediently listen to God. That's what James said. He said that strife in the church is the result of deafness and disobedience. We're not listening to God. Therefore, we need to listen to God. But we must listen with our hearts as well as our ears, and we must listen in obedience.

If we can listen to the Holy Spirit through the book of James, He will present again the answers to our every dilemma. God's answer to the problem of human sin is in Scripture. It is everywhere in the Word of God, so it will be in the last two chapters of James. But we must listen with new ears. We must, with Paul, let go of the past, "forgetting those things which are behind and reaching forward to those things which are ahead." We must look neither to the past nor to the future, but to God's Word and "press toward the goal for the prize of the upward call of God in Christ Jesus" (Philippians 3:13-14).

Listen to verses 9-10 again.

> "Lament and mourn and weep! Let your laughter be turned to mourning and your joy to gloom. Humble yourselves in the sight of the Lord, and He will lift you up."

The Lord Himself will lift us up.

We do not live in a season of celebration. God's church is in shambles! Oh, some churches look okay from the outside, but inside they are foul and corrupt. Before the celebration there is a season of mourning. God's celebration will come, but for now let us mourn together. Let us confess our faults together in prayer and repentance. This is a very important part of drawing near to God. If we are going to be lifted up—the promise of verse ten—we must first mourn and lament. Our potential joy must yield to sorrow and gloom for a time.

Christians need to humble themselves enough to admit the truth of their brokenness and failure before a watching world. We need to humble ourselves enough to allow ourselves to be where God's Word has brought us. We need to humble ourselves and listen to the Word of God. We need to humble ourselves in repentance.

Judging Others

Do not speak evil of one another, brethren. He who speaks evil of a brother and judges his brother, speaks evil of the law and judges the law. But if you judge the law, you are not a doer of the law but a judge. There is one Lawgiver, who is able to save and to destroy. Who are you to judge another? Come now, you who say, "Today or tomorrow we will go to such and such a city, spend a year there, buy and sell, and make a profit;" whereas you do not know what will happen tomorrow. For what is your life? It is even a vapor that appears for a little time and then vanishes away. Instead you ought to say, "If the Lord wills, we shall live and do this or that." But now you boast in your arrogance. All such boasting is evil. Therefore, to him who knows to do good and does not do it, to him it is sin.
—James 4:11-17

S am had recently joined the church and the pastor sought to help him get involved.

"I only have one talent," lamented Sam.

"And what is that?" asked the pastor.

"The talent of judging others. I'm an excellent judge of character."

The pastor thought for a moment and replied, "Well, I advise you to do with your talent what the man with one talent in the Bible did with his (Matthew 25:18)—bury it, because your one talent contradicts Scripture. Only God knows the secrets of a man's heart."

> "For the word of God is living and powerful, and sharper than any two-edged sword, piercing even to the division of soul and spirit, and of joints and marrow, and is a discerner of the thoughts and intents of the heart" (Hebrews 4:12).

Many Christians make this same error by claiming to be good judges of character. But inasmuch as people live as if they are, they live contrary to Scripture. James said, "He who judges his brother... judges the law" of God (v. 11). When we evaluate the actions or intentions of others by our own criteria, we set ourselves above God's law. That's a serious charge.

There has been much said about the scriptural admonition against judging others. It is used with force and is repeated often to control the parameters of what is politically correct. For instance, people are cautioned not to judge homosexuals or alcoholics. The caution contains a double innuendo. It calls into question our right to judge others, and it questions the judgment of God set out in Scripture, and His right to judge. It does all of this in the hope or belief that God is universally merciful, that all will be saved regardless of their behavior. The result of this faulty message is that otherwise faithful Christians stand by, passive and mute, as they watch their families and friends fall into sinful behavior—all the while thinking that their silence is an act of faithfulness to God.

James points out the folly of this kind of thinking. The whole of the book of James is a diatribe against the false thinking that drives the sins of the tongue. James listed those sins: being too fast or too willing to tell others what you think (James 1:19), evaluating the intentions of others (James 3:9), boasting (James 4:13), grumbling (James 5:9), and swearing (James 5:12). Gordon Keddie observes, "James' purpose is to show us what it means to be humbled before God as it applies to the way we speak of others when they are not there to hear what is said."[1] James' intent is to apply Scripture in a practical way to everyday life.

Do not speak evil or slander one another. The Greek word (katalaleo) means "to speak against." Its use in Scripture is often associated with the grumbling of God's people against their leaders (i.e., Psalm 78:19, 2 Corinthians 12:20, Romans 1:30). When ancient Israel wandered in the desert there was much grumbling against Moses and Aaron, and against the provision of the Lord. Moses' response is instructive, "Your complaints are not against us but against the Lord" (Exodus 16:8). They were unhappy with Moses' leadership, but Moses was only following orders, God's orders.

---

1   Keddie, p. 166.

Sometimes we think that faithfulness would be much easier if God would just appear and tell us what He wants us to do. We console ourselves by thinking that we would simply obey Him, were that to happen. But I beg to differ, or rather Scripture begs to differ because God *has* appeared in Christ. God has already expressed His will regarding everything that ultimately matters. Yet, many people have not found it easier to obey, but more difficult. The problem isn't so much that people don't understand God's will, but that they don't like it.

"The law of the Lord is perfect, converting the soul; The testimony of the Lord is sure, making wise the simple" (Psalms 19:7). Advanced degrees are not necessary to understand Scripture. But conversion is required. The purpose of Scripture is to convert the soul. The unconverted struggle against God's Word until they are converted, at which time they grow in understanding and appreciation of it. The implication of this verse is that those who complain of not knowing God's will or not understanding God's Word are struggling with their own conversion.

But that does not mean that everyone who is unclear about God's will is unsaved. I personally know that regeneration happens in an instant—like birth. But it is not completed in an instant. Salvation is a life-long endeavor. Being born again doesn't mean that you automatically understand God's Word or will. Infants do not understand English from the womb. Knowledge of God, like knowledge of language, requires time and effort. So, don't expect to get it if you are not putting forth the effort. The adage, "use it or lose it," also applies. Not that you can lose real salvation, but if the fruits of repentance are not yours, you are probably fooling yourself about having it in the first place.

JUDGING OTHERS

We are all naturally inclined to judge one another. It is a natural part of life. Judging others even has an appropriate place in God's kingdom. But there is a false understanding of this scriptural injunction against judging others that is in wide circulation today. Sinners often use it to keep Christians at bay, to keep them from pronouncing God's judgment on their particular sins.

"Who are you to judge?" people often retort when their sin is exposed. "You have no right to judge me or anyone else until you get your own life straightened out." I'm sure you have heard such arguments. They are often used by the homosexual and recovery group communities to keep the judgment of the church at bay. The argument is that "as long as you are guilty of sin yourself, you have no right to say anything to anyone." And like most of Satan's lies this one is mostly true. It is true that we are all sinners, and it is true that we have no right to judge anyone else. But that doesn't mean that nothing should be said.

We all have a tendency to think that everyone else should live by *our* standards. When we judge others we impose our standards on them. And when that happens people object, as they should. Just as we object when we are judged because we don't do things the way someone else does. We rationalize, "If I believe I'm right about something and I want to be helpful to someone else, then I should do what I can to help him to do it my way because my way is the right way." That's a fine line of thinking until someone tries to use it on *me*!

That kind of judging shouldn't be done. The politically correct pundits are correct about that. But is that the kind of judging that Scripture talks about? It is *part* of what Scripture talks about, and James agrees that it should not be done.

But there is another kind of judging discussed in Scripture. It is called *discernment*. There really isn't much difference between discernment and judging. They have similar definitions. And yet biblical discernment is the prized possession of the wise. Wisdom requires discernment—judging. How do we know when to judge and when not to judge? Or how to judge?

The wisdom of discernment requires the use of God's judgment, not our own. We are not to judge others—or anything for that matter—according to our own subjective values, not according to what we think is right or wrong. Rather, Christians are to employ God's judgment, according to what the Bible teaches about right and wrong. It's not that all judgment is to be suspended because of God's grace and mercy. But because human judgment is always sinful, Christians must rely upon God's judgment, the judgment of Scripture.

In fact, it is the obligation of the church, of Christians gathered in worship, to exercise God's judgment. And, of course, the best way to do that is to apply it to ourselves first. The first thing that all sinners are commanded to do is to apply God's judgment to themselves. We must each and all hold ourselves up to the standards of the Bible and allow God's judgment to fall upon us. Unless the sting of God's judgment is felt personally, there can be no real conviction of sin, no repentance, no regeneration, no new life.

We often fail to hold ourselves accountable to God's standards, so God has ordained others to help us—not because God wants to boost His self-esteem by imposing His will upon helpless creatures, but because living by God's judgment and God's values promotes human health and happiness more than anything else.

God's calling is a high calling, and people don't always want to be held responsible to God's standards. It is a difficult row to hoe. But because it is good for us, God has provided help along the way. We are to help one another maintain God's standards. God has ordained particular authorities to help us in this regard—fellow believers, parents, church leaders, and civil governments. When we fail to live up to God's best for us, those who have authority over us are to provide appropriate help.

The first line of that help is to provide a clear understanding of God's standard. We need to know what God expects. You don't need to know what I think, and I don't need to know what you think. What you and I think is irrelevant. But it is important for us to know what God has said about the matter. And that has been given in Scripture.

Part of the difficulty with Scripture is that the contemporary world believes that all truth is relative, that all values are a matter of personal interpretation. And inasmuch as we speak of human values or standards, that is true. All our thoughts are relative to one another—and relatively unimportant.

But there is an exception to general relativity. That exception is God's Word. God's Word is not relative, but absolute. It is the Rock of salvation. It is the Foundation Stone. It is eternal and cannot be shaken. It is infallible and sufficient for its purpose. It is ever the same and unchanging. It is absolute. And the absolute truth of the Word of God —Scripture interpreted by Scripture in the community of the faithful— is to be shared among Christians and proclaimed to the world. The absolute truth of Scripture is a matter of life and death. No kidding!

REVIEW

What have I said in this paraphrase of James? I said that we should not apply our own standards of behavior to others. We shouldn't judge others. Rather, we are obligated as Christians to apply God's Word and

His judgment to ourselves first and foremost, to agree with His judgment that we are all guilty sinners. We are then to share God's judgments against sin and expectations of human behavior with one another in Christian fellowship. And finally, as a church we are to proclaim God's absolute truth and God's judgment to the world, without guile, anger, or self-righteousness.

Finally, but not least importantly, we are to submit ourselves to the authorities that God has ordained over us. We are to submit in Christ to fellow believers, parents, church leaders, and governments. It is not our place to judge others. But it is our place to live according to God's judgment ourselves.

God's Future

*Come now, you who say, "Today or tomorrow we will go to such
and such a city, spend a year there, buy and sell, and make a profit;"
whereas you do not know what will happen tomorrow. For what is
your life? It is even a vapor that appears for a little time and then
vanishes away. Instead you ought to say, "If the Lord wills, we shall
live and do this or that." But now you boast in your arrogance. All
such boasting is evil. Therefore, to him who knows to do good and
does not do it, to him it is sin.*   —James 4:13-17

Contemporary people are driven by their passion for the future.
Every aspect of our lives is affected by it. We are inundated
with desk planners, wall planners, menu planners, Christmas
clubs, retirement plans, and a vast array of assorted payment plans for the
swelling debt that is rising like spring flood waters. Debt itself requires a
commitment to the future, and Americans are in debt to the hilt.

Vast amounts of time and energy are consumed by our incessant
planning for the future. We spend more time planning for the future or
pinning for the past than we do living in the present. Meanwhile, life
slips by unnoticed, and often unlived.

Don't get me wrong, it is wise and prudent to plan for the future
and prepare for various contingencies. Scripture does not call us to
ignore the future. In fact, Scripture insists that believers make careful
preparation for the future, both long and short term. James is not calling
Christians to discount God's future. He simply provides a caution.

People want to be like God, who alone knows the end from the
beginning. But such knowledge is the prerogative of God alone. Sure,
God occasionally let the Old Testament prophets in on His plans, but

that has never been a norm among His people. Rather, it is the good fortune of Christians (actually of God's will), *not* to know the future, but to trust the Lord, who alone knows the future.

But planning for the future is not James' point. The issue that James was concern about is our attitude about the future. The problem is that when people are fully assured that the future will go according to their plans, they have gone beyond human limitations, and have presumed on the providence of God. "There are many plans in a man's heart, Nevertheless the Lord's counsel—that will stand" (Proverbs 19:21). Human plans do not always (and perhaps seldom) agree with God's providence. History is littered with the wreckage of great human plans.

The difficulty is not with making plans, we all need to make plans for the future. The problem is not understanding God's Word or God's will, in spite of the fact that it is laid out in Scripture. The problem is that Christians too often subvert the blessings of their own faith.

James is talking about the sin of presumption. To presume is to overstep one's bounds or limits. It is the taking of something or someone for granted. We who are married know well the dangers of taking our spouse for granted. It is probably the greatest source of marital conflict. The same thing is true regarding our relationship with God. It is so easy to presume upon the Lord, whatever we think He wants for us.

PRESUMPTION

A young man fell in love with a woman at Bible college. Like many young Christians, he was headstrong for the Lord. One day he shared with her the "fact" that the Lord told him that they were to be married.

"Really," she replied. "The Lord has told me nothing of the kind. And, as it stands right now we are definitely not going to get married at all!"

He was devastated with her reply. They never did marry. He presumed that His desires were God's will.

Keddie says, "It is possible to baptize our inward convictions with the certainty of divine decree when in fact we are fooling ourselves."[1] That was James' concern.

---

1   Keddie, p. 177.

"The heart is deceitful above all things, And desperately wicked; Who can know it?" (Jeremiah 17:9), lamented Jeremiah. Jeremiah's point was that people are very susceptible to self-delusion. Well meaning Christians to often confuse their own fervent beliefs and desires with the will of God. This practice is not unusual. It is too common.

The arrival of the Third Millennium has brought a rash of so-called Bible predictions and prophecies about the will of God. How many times has the end of the world been predicted before? How many times has a specific date been prophesied for Jesus' return? Or a particular end-times scenario been attached to a particular politician or world event? How many people think that they speak for God?

Too many!

But this malady doesn't just affect self-appointed end-time prophets. It affects many ordinary Christians in pulpits and pews alike. It is all too common to presumptuously attribute divine providence to our own hopes and dreams—for ourselves, for our families, even for our churches. Presumption is like a cancer, causing an uncontrollable multiplication of a particular kind of cell. Cancer is an unrestrained growth that ultimately leads to death. James was simply raising a flag of caution about the dangers of presumption. It is contagious.

James describes the error of planning apart from God's providence in verse 13. Verse 14 offers the caution that life is short and uncertain. He then concludes chapter four with an exhortation of practical dependence upon God's providence (vs. 15-17).

In spite of all our plans, we don't really know what will happen even tomorrow. "For what is your life? ...a vapor that appears for a little time and then vanishes away" (v. 14). Scripture everywhere teaches that we cannot depend on our own future plans, but that we must trust in God's care and provision.

Christians are to be confident in the Lord. We are to trust the Lord, and seek the assurance of faithfulness. But assurance of faith is not a blank check from God for whatever we want, not even for what we think is right! We must hope—it's part of being faithfu. But we must depend on God, not on our own hopes. Our hope is not to be self-directed, but God-directed.

TRUSTING IN GOD'S FUTURE

Jesus told a parable that illustrates this (Luke 12:16-21). "The ground of a certain rich man yielded plentifully." It had a history of yielding plentifully in the past. "And he thought within himself, saying, 'What shall I do, since I have no room to store my crops?'" The man's first mistake was that he counted on his harvest before he had it. Good crops are never guaranteed.

"So he said, 'I will do this: I will pull down my barns and build greater, and there I will store all my crops and my goods.'" His second mistake was to think that he could take care of himself. Building a bigger barn was no guarantee of a good harvest. Neither does a good harvest guarantee a prosperous life.

"And I will say to my soul, 'Soul, you have many goods laid up for many years; take your ease; eat, drink, and be merry.'" His third mistake, related to his second, was to believe that the future would be just like the past, that he could accurately anticipate the future.

"But God said to him, 'Fool! This night your soul will be required of you; then whose will those things be which you have provided?'" Jesus gave us a lesson about thinking that we can anticipate and provide for our own future. "So is he who lays up treasure for himself, and is not rich toward God." The lesson is more than not counting your chickens before they hatch. It is not trusting in yourself, or in your society, but trusting in God's providence.

James exhortation in verses 15-17 concludes with a three-step process for proper dependence upon God. First, always maintain a kind of holy tentativeness (v. 15). Second, meet life with genuine humility (v. 16). And third, be willing to obey the Lord in all things (v. 17).

EVERY STEP

There is a popular but false belief afoot in modern evangelicalism. It concerns the biblical principle of eternal security and its corollary, the assurance of faith. It falsely believes that real Christians must have a kind of tremendous confidence about everything in life. It encourages a kind of divine presumption that finds God's direction in every circumstance. And while it is true that God guides the faithful, the false teaching is that to fail to believe that the Lord directs one's every step means the loss of one's assurance of faith.

I don't want to throw doubt upon God's providence for His people, because it is true that God cares for His people in a myriad of ways, most of which we are unaware. But there is a kind of presumption that many people have about God's care and providence that tends to rationalize their own personal desires. It goes like this, "God allowed me to win the bingo jackpot the other night, and with that win I have exactly enough for the down payment on that ruby red Toyota I've been eyeing. Therefore, it is God's will that I buy the car I want." Such thinking is nonsense.

There is a self-serving attitude at the root of such presumption. That self-serving attitude is what James was trying to expose to the light of reason. Just because Scripture proves that God is very specific in caring for His people, doesn't mean that every thought that occurs to born again Christians is a "word from the Lord." In fact, well-meaning, genuine, born again Christians can simply be plain wrong in their thinking—with no reflection on the ultimate status of their eternal salvation!

Rather, James argues, it is much more in keeping with Scripture to approach life—not with doubt, but with caution or tentativeness, particularly when it pertains to God's will. Yes, God's will is clear in Scripture. But God's will for our own individual lives is not so easy to discern. It is much easier to look back upon the past (history) and see how God has directed and sustained us in particular ways. It is much more difficult in the midst of the ebb and flow of life to determine exactly what God's will is regarding a particular matter. Again, the difficulty is that we often get our own desires mixed in with our understanding of God's will. This is a very common problem.

James suggests that such confusion leads to a kind of bragging confidence that justifies itself in the name of the Lord. To have the unquestionable confidence that the Lord God Almighty directs your every step and decision can produce a self-deceiving arrogance. Again, I'm not saying that God doesn't watch over every aspect of our lives. His eye is indeed on the sparrow. He numbers the very hairs on our heads. All of that is true.

But for a person to then believe that he can, therefore, absolutely know God's will because "He watches over me" is a huge mistake. Or to believe that a particular thought is indubitably from God can too easily lead to self-delusion and temerity. For me to believe with all of my heart that some particular decision is absolutely from God—a decision not yet proven by history, to believe that I absolutely know God's will —leaves no room for sin and human error. No room even for God Himself to correct me!

"No!" says James. "That kind of thinking is too likely to produce a false confidence that presumes upon God."

Finally, James brings this thought to a conclusion by suggesting that "obedience to the *known will of God* is the exclusive path of personal holiness."[2] Truth and obedience must always go together. They cannot be separated without a loss of integrity. This is not the doctrine that personal holiness produces salvation. Rather, it is the doctrine that salvation produces an increase in personal holiness.

Understanding more of God's truth always requires increasing obedience to the truth already given. If we fail in our obedience, God will not trust any additional truth to us. The converse is also true regarding obedience. If we find ourselves disobedient, we must correct our disobedience, not with an increase of the raw will to obey, but through greater understanding of God's truth, through Bible study.

The key for this process to work is understanding that the known will of God can only be discovered in Scripture. Through the study of Scripture alone Christians can learn God's principles (doctrines) for life. Those principles, then, inasmuch as we fully understand them, will truly guide us according to God's will as we apply them to our particular situations. But like medicine, it is more an art that requires practice, than a hard science of formulas and predictable results.

RECAP

What did James say? He advised Christians not to trust their own thoughts or feelings, but to trust God alone through Christ alone accor4ding to Scripture alone because the future belongs to God alone, and therefore, the precise details of the future cannot be known by us with certainty in this life.

This is not to say that God's future cannot be known at all, or that we cannot have confidence in God's certain victory. Indeed, the future can be known because God told us in Scripture about His plan to save His people from certain destruction. But we do not, and cannot know

---

2   Keddie p. 181, italics added.

the details about how God's plan will unfold before time—much less the details of our ordinary, individual futures.

FATTENED HEARTS

*Come now, you rich, weep and howl for your miseries that are
coming upon you! Your riches are corrupted, and your garments are
moth-eaten. Your gold and silver are corroded, and their corrosion
will be a witness against you and will eat your flesh like fire. You
have heaped up treasure in the last days. Indeed the wages of the
laborers who mowed your fields, which you kept back by fraud, cry
out; and the cries of the reapers have reached the ears of the Lord of
Sabaoth. You have lived on the earth in pleasure and luxury; you
have fattened your hearts as in a day of slaughter. You have
condemned, you have murdered the just; he does not resist you.*
—James 5:1-6

From the beginning James has been speaking a word of judgment
against the many sins and infractions of the wealthy against the
poor. Siding with the poor, James began chapter one by espous-
ing the Christian benefits of trials and tribulations. Difficulties are a natural part of life, and James pointed out God's providence and care for
His people in spite of difficulties in the world. Sometimes the difficulties
themselves are part of God's providential care for His people. Sometimes
God provides circumstances that His people call *difficulties*, but He calls
them *blessings*. Consequently, James calls Christians to love God even—
and especially—in the midst of difficulties.

He went on to caution Christians against favoritism, against prefer-
ring some people above others, particularly in the sense of confusing our
own likes and dislikes with the judgments or values of God. God has His
own reasons for doing what He does, and we are not privy to God's

intentions. God does not need to consult with us about His judgments, or make them understandable to us. He is self-sufficient.

James warned us about the dangers of our own limited judgments and their expression as he spoke of the untamable tongue. We sin with our tongues because we sin in our thoughts and beliefs about God, and about other people. James pointed out the total depravity—the moral poverty and utter sinfulness—of mankind. And because of our sinful depravity, we cannot rely upon human wisdom, but must depend on God's wisdom alone.

Chapter four pointed out the many problems that occur when people don't rely on God's wisdom. James demonstrated that strife and conflict were sure indications of rampant pride and selfishness, and the failure to live by God's righteousness—and particularly when such things occur in churches. As Christ humbled Himself, not only before God, but before His accusers as well, so we are to humble ourselves before God, before Christ, and even before one another.

Not only are Christians forbidden to use their own judgment (their own personal likes, dislikes, and understandings) to evaluate others, they are also to refrain from trying to make judgments about what the future will bring. Rather, we are to employ God's judgment, and to apply it primarily to ourselves and our own lifestyles. Similarly we are to trust in God's provision for the future, and not trust our own projections and plans. In everything we are to simply rely upon the Lord.

In chapter five James made the case that the wealthy are the most likely to sin against God and their fellow man in the ways he has described. Please understand that Scripture is not opposed to wealth per se, but stands adamantly opposed to its abuse. James suggests that the wealthy are most likely to abuse wealth only because they have it. But the poor are not absolved from similar sins. The poor often abuse wealth as well by neglecting God's injunctions regarding work and frugality. In chapter five James takes aim at the abuses of the wealthy against the poor, a familiar theme of Scripture.

The repetition of "weep and howl" (or "wail," v. 1) emphasizes that sorrow and grief will be great indeed for those who fail to live by God's precepts. God's warnings always concern His future judgment. And the judgment here isn't about one's verbal commitment to Christ, but about actions and lifestyles. James is concerned that people's lives reflect their verbal commitments. James has argued previously that verbal commitment alone is not adequate. He means that actions speak louder than words, that a faith commitment that is devoid of faithful expressions of love and a genuine Christian lifestyle is not a real commitment. And, therefore, such professed faith cannot be genuine faith.

He has argued that we must not trust in our own plans for the future, nor, by implication, in "gold and silver" (v. 3), the stuff of the world. However, the poor are just as likely to trust in gold and silver as the wealthy, though in a different way. The wealthy trust in it by hoarding it because they believe that it will save them by providing for their rainy day needs. The poor, on the other hand, often worship wealth every bit as much as the rich. The only difference is that they don't have it. But if they did, they would be in the same situation, committing similar sins. As it is, they sin by lusting in their hearts for the wealth they don't have.

James' point is that wealth itself exerts a strong influence toward worldly corruption and sin—not always, but far too often. Scripture is very adamant in its condemnation of materialism—selfishness, greed, and worldliness. Calvin said, "all those are generally condemned who unjustly accumulate riches, or who foolishly abuse them."[1] Generally speaking, the rich hoard money, while the poor foolishly manage it.

An argument can be made that the judgment alluded to here pertained to the destruction of the Temple in A.D. 70. No doubt, that was part of God's judgment against the unfaithfulness of Israel that had accumulated over the centuries. But there is no reason to assume that the destruction of the Temple constituted the whole of God's end time judgment. Life and history continued beyond A.D. 70.

Just as the advent of Christ began the end times of the New Testament era, the return of Jesus will bring God's judgment to a climax. Just as the beginning of God's end time judgment was marked by the destruction of the Temple, so the climax of the New Testament era will be marked by other great judgments, particularly the judgment of each individual before the eternal throne of God.

Against this judgment James employs the counsel of the Psalmist:

> "A little that a righteous man has Is better than the riches of
> many wicked. For the arms of the wicked shall be broken, But
> the Lord upholds the righteous" (Psalm 37:16-17).

---

1   *Calvin's Commentaries*, Vol. XXII, Baker Book House, 1993, p. 344.

The bottom line of the Lord's Word regarding wealth is always to be content with what you have. But that doesn't mean to be content with poverty. The Lord doesn't want His people to be poor. He wants them to work hard, to be compensated fairly for their work, and to be responsible stewards of what they have.

The peculiar sins that James was concerned with are provided in verses 4-5. Beyond repentance (rethinking and rearranging our lives to better conform to God's Word), sinners have only two alternatives. They can either sin boldly by ignoring God's counsel, or they can rationalize their behavior by redefining sin in such a way that they do not understand themselves to commit it. Generally speaking, atheists choose to sin boldly, and hypocrites redefine sin.

FRAUD

James also alludes to a failure to pay fair wages. The details of the situation are neither available nor necessary. The means by which the wealthy have not paid their employees are not given in the NIV, "The wages you failed to pay the workmen who mowed your fields are crying out against you." The NIV consistently slurs references to particular sins. Whereas the NKJV (following the older KJV) reads,

> "Indeed the wages of the laborers who mowed your fields, *which you kept back by fraud*, cry out; and the cries of the reapers have reached the ears of the Lord of Hosts" (v. 4, italics added).

From the laborers' perspective it doesn't matter why they haven't been paid, it is enough that they didn't receive what was owed them. But God, seeking to correct the sin of the wealthy, identified their particular sin. Note that the Bible often seeks to convict people through the clear identification of particular sins, of which they themselves are guilty. Consequently, the older translations are to be preferred here.

Fraud is an important issue because the wealthy not only defraud the poor of their wages, but they defraud God of the glory that is His, which would be provided through a right relationship with Him. To commit fraud means to pretend to be someone you aren't. In relationship to God fraud means that people pretend to be other than what God knows them to be. The denial of personal sin is at issue, and the denial of personal sin and its fraud loom large in contemporary society. People generally do not see themselves as sinners. Consequently, they excuse themselves from a saving relationship with God on the grounds that if they are not sinners, they don't need Jesus!

But the denial of sin affects more than the rich. Lots of people defraud God by refusing to admit that He is right about their sin. The trouble is that wealth makes that kind of fraud easier to commit because it provides both means and motive for the denial of sin. The motive is greed—keeping what you already have. And money itself provides the means. People are afraid that God wants their money, that taking Christ seriously will have a significant effect upon their pocketbook. And they are right! Taking the faith seriously will impact how we live and how we spend our money. If it doesn't, we should question our own faith.

Nonetheless, God doesn't actually want our money. He wants *His* money. God is the creator and owner of everything. Consequently, He is the creator of money and wealth as well. Everything belongs to God. So, God doesn't want *our* money because we don't own any. Rather, by His grace and mercy He allows us to keep ninety percent for ourselves, our families, and our personal concerns. But the other ten percent is His to do with what He wants. At the very least, God wants His tithe.

God's church becomes weak and anemic when His people starve it by withholding what is rightfully His. Imagine the vital ministries churches would have if their budgets doubled. If all Christians tithed, church budgets would likely increase at lease three or four times.

HEART DISEASE

Heart disease is the number one killer of Americans. The causes are many, but surely diet is a major factor. Fast food is fat food. It's quick and easy. Quick and easy always appeal to a deeper dis-ease of the heart. Jeremiah said that the heart is wicked. Part of its wickedness is the desire for quick and easy solutions to life's problems. The American appetite for fast food is symptomatic of a deeper desire for a quick-and-easy, instant lifestyle that plays fast and loose with God's mandates. It began with Eve in the Garden.

In contrast, Scripture offers no quick and easy solutions to anything. Rather, it offers eternal salvation. God is in it for the long haul. His ways are slow and steady compared to the world. But His results are lasting and sustainable—eternal. While the world offers quick and easy solutions, God offers Christ's eternal faithfulness in the midst of a sinful

and wicked world. If the Bible teaches anything it teaches patience in
the face of disappointment, not the passing satisfaction of quick fixes.

We live in the midst of the "pleasure and luxury" (v. 5) of the
twentieth century, where hearts grow fat, restricting the flow of blood
and life. The similarities between physical heart disease and spiritual
heart dis-ease are astonishing. Quick-fix spiritual diets rob hearts of
many of the spiritual nutrients needed for abundant, long-lasting life.
The spiritual heart of contemporary society has grown dangerously
weak from a poor diet and lack of spiritual exercise.

The blessing that James offers begins with a crash course in reality
therapy. He does not offer hope to fat-ladened hearts, but condemns
them by the Word of God. Such condemnation is a wake-up call. The
wake-up call is rightly communicated through condemnation. Eliminate the condemnation, and you eliminate the urgency of the wake-up
call. The only real hope of the gospel is to make sure that God's wake-
up call is heard and headed. Consequently, James allows the condemnation to stand because it constitutes a blessing in the long run.

Because faith begins in repentance, and repentance begins in conviction of sin, James condemns sinners in the most direct way possible.
God's purpose is to heal or purify the fattened hearts of His people who
have gorged themselves on quick-fix spirituality and dozed off in a spiritual stupor.

If you find this message disturbing, in all probability the discomfort
that you feel is the urgency of God's wake-up call. Don't blame me, the
message is not mine. I'm just the messenger. If, on the other hand, you
don't find this message particularly disturbing, you are probably fast
asleep.

James ends this section of his letter with a bold accusation. Speaking to his readers—the church. He said, "you have murdered the just"
(v. 6). He means Christians like you and me. We murder justice and
righteousness by ignoring the message of the gospel, and the fact that
we do it *in the churches* serves to make our guilt and sin all the more
serious. We stand convicted before the Lord—you and me! The stupor
of sleep cannot absolve us of our guilt. Our only option is to accept the
just condemnation awaiting us at God's bar of justice. We simply must
face our guilt and turn to Christ.

Its time to cut to the chase.

BE PATIENT

Therefore be patient, brethren, until the coming of the Lord. See how the farmer waits for the precious fruit of the earth, waiting patiently for it until it receives the early and latter rain. You also be patient. Establish your hearts, for the coming of the Lord is at hand. Do not grumble against one another, brethren, lest you be condemned. Behold, the Judge is standing at the door! My brethren, take the prophets, who spoke in the name of the Lord, as an example of suffering and patience. Indeed we count them blessed who endure. You have heard of the perseverance of Job and seen the end intended by the Lord—that the Lord is very compassionate and merciful.
—James 5:7-11

James now returns to his original theme, bringing his letter to a four-part conclusion. His conclusion calls for patience (vs. 7-11), prayer and praise (vs. 12-13), fellowship (vs. 14-18), and diligent ministry (vs. 19-20). We will begin by looking at the purpose of godly patience.

The classic prayer for patience is, "Lord, give me patience, and give it to me now!" We all need patience because we don't have enough. By nature Americans are impatient. Our technological success has increased our need for patience because technology continues to allow us to do things faster and faster. Consequently, we find ourselves growing more and more impatient when we don't get what we want right away.

Computers provide an appropriate example. A new computer can make the old one seem ever so slow, although it seemed fast enough when we first got it. The same is true with microwaves. Having gotten used to heating a cup of tea in a minute, I find myself champing at the bit if I have to wait for the tea kettle to boil on the stove.

James' call to patience refers back to chapter one.

> "My brethren, count it all joy when you fall into various trials, knowing that the testing of your faith produces patience. But let patience have its perfect work, that you may be perfect and complete, lacking nothing" (James 1:2-4).

However, he now calls to mind the one thing that gives patience stability—"the coming of the Lord" (v. 5). It is the anticipation of the second coming, in conjunction with the knowledge that we will meet Christ at death, that anchors Godly patience.

We must not get distracted by the human goals and expectations that we may have for God's church. Rather, faithfulness requires that we set our eyes and hearts upon Christ's return. Inasmuch as we get sidetracked by our own thoughts and plans we can easily circumvent God's plans. It is so easy to get ahead of the Lord.

> "The Lord is not slack (or slow) concerning His promise, as some count slackness, but is long-suffering toward us, not willing that any should perish but that all should come to repentance" (2 Peter 3:9).

We often find ourselves getting frustrated with God's timing. We know what we want, and we want it now!

"What's the matter with God? Can't He see what is needed?"

We assume that is why He needs us, and we enlist ourselves to help the Lord get something done. But too often we get ahead of the Lord, having convinced ourselves that what He wants is what we want. It is the old sin of presumption rearing its head again.

BLACKSMITH AND FARMER

When a blacksmith works on a piece of iron He first holds it in the fire until it gets white-hot. Impatience at this initial phase of blacksmithing will make the work much more difficult, if not impossible. To be most pliable, the iron must be white-hot. It must be the same for the Lord as He makes us pliable by holding us in the heat of trials and tribulations. Then at the height of our heat, He holds us to His anvil and hammers us into the shape He desires. We must realize that God is shaping us to His specifications. We are not supposed to shape ourselves to suit ourselves.

James holds before us three examples of patience—the farmer, the prophets, and the patriarch Job. The farmer in days of old was helpless before the forces of nature. He could only plow and plant. He was completely dependent upon the Lord for rain. He could only wait for the early and the latter rain. The two rainy seasons suggests that spiritual work, like farming, involves a process. There are seasons to spiritual growth. Without the early rain the seed would not sprout, without the latter rain it would not ripen.

The farmer does not cause the crops to grow. God is the source of growth. The farmer's responsibility is to plant and till. The growth or increase comes from God. A farmer can do everything in his power, and still have a poor harvest. So it is with God's church. There are more factors involved in healthy church growth than we can account for. Healthy church growth does not depend upon human ability. Churches are not only dependent upon their own times and seasons, but are absolutely dependent upon God's grace. Paul "planted, Apollos watered, but God gave the increase" (1 Corinthians 3:6).

Once the field has been plowed and planted, the farmer must wait. Waiting upon the Lord is not a matter of passivity, but of patience. We must realize that we are not waiting for this or that particular plant (or church) to bloom and grow. We are, rather, waiting for the harvest. We are waiting for Christ to usher in the New Kingdom. Success is a great experience, but we must not get sidetracked by passing phenomena. Sure, we'd like a successful church. But a church that is successful by the world's standards does not further God's Kingdom.

In fact, success itself can become a great obstacle to God's truth. There is no greater gospel distraction than worldly success. All too often success by the world's measure provides interference with the genuine reception of the gospel of grace. Too often, those who have gained worldly success—the success of numbers, i.e., dollars, sales, membership, attendance—have little time for or interest in the grace and joy of admonishment at the hand of the Lord. They often think they don't need it, or that they don't need it now, or that things don't really work that way, or that their success proves that they already have God's blessing. So, they excuse themselves from God's discipline because they think they have better things to do with their time.

James counsels us to use patience to "establish our hearts" (v. 8). To establish, *sterizo*, means to make stable, to strengthen, or to render constant. It means that

> "we should no longer be children, tossed to and fro and carried about with every wind of doctrine, by the trickery of men, in the cunning craftiness of deceitful plotting, but, speaking the truth in love, may grow up in all things into Him who is the head—Christ—from whom the whole body, joined and knit together by what every joint supplies, according to the effective working by which every part does its share, causes growth of the body for the edifying of itself in love" (Ephesians 4:14-16).

This kind of gospel stability—being truly and solidly established in Christ—produces genuine spiritual growth. Here is God's recommendation for church growth—not multiple services, not having the "right" pastor, not a new building, not a special kind of music, but the personal establishment of each church member in Christ.

However, by the same token, just because some church is growing numerically doesn't necessarily mean that their members are established in Christ according to Scripture. God doesn't work by formulas, but by grace and His own free will. Maturity often produces growth, but it doesn't guarantee growth.

Scripture says that we "should no longer be children, (no longer) be tossed to and fro... (no longer) carried about with every wind of doctrine" (Ephesians 4:14) The clear implication is that Christians are actually quite vulnerable to such things. People are always more easily influenced by fads than by truth. The gospel was never a fad, never popular in the sense that it is today. And when it becomes popular you can be sure that it is misunderstood. Numerical success has never been God's measure, nor should it be ours.

Rather, the measure of God's success is found in our readiness to meet the Lord today. "The coming of the Lord is at hand" (v. 8) and we must be ready. As the hymnist writes:

Jesus is coming to earth again, What if it were today?
Coming in power and love to reign, What if it were today?
Coming to claim His chosen Bride, All the redeemed and purified,

Over this whole earth scattered wide, What if it were today?[1]

The Lord knows that being a Christian is a high calling, and because it is a high calling, it brings struggle and frustration. We know this because struggle and frustration are often addressed in Scripture. Everywhere in the New Testament church we find struggle and trouble. James dealt extensively with this theme. He offered counsel regarding favoritism, gossip, slander, false wisdom, pride, and boasting. It is a struggle to be who Christ called us to be.

James went on, "Do not grumble against one another, brethren, lest you be condemned" (v. 9). Patience and understanding are part of the calling of every Christian. Christians must be able to disagree without bickering and disputing—without breaking fellowship. Christians must seek God's orderly and honorable way to resolve the problem of differing opinions.

A good model is to share our own best thinking and insights together in humility, and then submit to God's ordained (called and elected) leadership. People are generally able to do that—as long as things go their way. But James calls Christians to a higher standard than that. James calls Christians to *want* what God wants, not to pretend that our desires are God's desires, but to make God's desires our desires.

He calls attention to the prophets of old "who spoke in the name of the Lord, as an example of suffering and patience" (v. 10). None of the Old Testament Prophets were ever popular. Rather, each was hated and despised because God's truth did not agree with the popular wisdom of the day. The Prophets preached God's enduring truth in the face of unpopularity and were ridiculed and persecuted for it. Most of the Prophets came to an untimely demise. Their lives were full of struggle and persecution. Yet, they endured. They continued in their faithfulness in spite of the difficulties it brought them. That is the example that James calls us to emulate.

Finally, He lifts up the example of Job. In spite of Job's faithfulness, he lost everything—his farm, his health, and his family. Yet, he hung on to God's truth. As he began to experience loss, "his wife said to him, Do you still hold to your integrity? Curse God and die!" (Job 2:9). His own wife counseled him to forget God, to abandon his faith, to ignore God's

---

1   Words & Music: Lelia N. Morris, in *The King's Praises,* No. 3, Philadelphia, Pennsylvania: The Praise Publishing Company, 1912.

truth, and let nature take its course. But Job would not turn his back on the Lord. He admonished his wife and clung to his integrity, and to his faith.

That's our example. Admonish those who would have us turn away from God to the right or to the left. Admonish those who would have God hurry up or slow down. We must hold to the faith as did Job. We must hold to God's course, steady and sure, though it often seems so slow. We must persevere as did Job, even when we lose everything and there is no hope in sight. We must persevere, often against family and friends, and hold to the integrity of faithfulness.

When the whole world calls us to let go of what they call foolishness, but what God calls faithfulness, we must hold steady with patience and perseverance. Why is the Lord not slack concerning His promise, as some count slackness? Why is the Lord long-suffering toward us? Why is He not willing that any should perish? Because He seeks that all should come to repentance (2 Peter 3:9). Aren't you glad that God is patient with *you*? I'm glad He is patient with me. He's waiting for our repentance.

God is patient toward His people because He knows the importance of time. Should we be less patient toward one another? Should we in our impatience cut short the time that God is patiently using to bring His people to repentance? If *we* need God's patience with us, then so do others. And we must grant patience to others, lest God cut us short.

Think of the person that most irritates you, and consider that God has called that particular person to be near you in order to provide you with opportunities to exercise your fledgling patience. The very person who irritates you the most has been sent by God to help you grow in patience. God has given you that special opportunity with that particular person! Be thankful for it.

Prayer & Praise

*But above all, my brethren, do not swear, either by heaven or by earth
or with any other oath. But let your "Yes," be "Yes," and your "No,"
"No," lest you fall into judgment. Is anyone among you suffering?
Let him pray. Is anyone cheerful? Let him sing psalms.*

—James 5:12-13

In chapter one James offered a three-part, practical definition of true religion: 1) curbing the tongue, 2) helping widows and orphans, and 3) avoiding the corruption of the world, or moral purity. These are the manifestations of true religion. James knows that true religion cannot be gained by outward behavior, that it must first be a matter of inward conviction. The point is not that doing certain things will make a person religious, but that religious people do certain things because they want to please God.

As usual, James has a two-fold concern. He insists that the inner spiritual life of Christians manifest itself with integrity through their behavior. His concern is that Godly thoughts and Godly deeds be genuinely united in the hearts of Christians.

Cussing

James is concerned that the words that Christians speak always give honor and glory to God. And, inasmuch as speaking is simply an overflow of thinking, it is imperative that the thoughts that Christians think give honor and glory to God as well. He makes the point by reminding his readers of Christ's injunction not to swear.

> "Again you have heard that it was said to those of old, 'You shall not swear falsely, but shall perform your oaths to the Lord.' But I

say to you, do not swear at all: neither by heaven, for it is God's throne; nor by the earth, for it is His footstool; nor by Jerusalem, for it is the city of the great King. Nor shall you swear by your head, because you cannot make one hair white or black. But let your 'Yes' be 'Yes,' and your 'No,' 'No.' For whatever is more than these is from the evil one" (Matthew 5:33-37).

Swearing is a violation of the Third Commandment. Yet, in spite of Moses' injunction against it, swearing was common in Jesus' day, as it is in ours. Now, when Scripture speaks of swearing it doesn't simply mean using cuss words. Yes, cuss words should not be used, but there is much more to this Commandment than not using cuss words, although that's a good start.

We are not to use God's name in vain, in ways that are not authorized by Scripture. To use something "in vain" means to use it to no account. Nothing comes of it, or nothing helpful comes of it. Vanity is emptiness, futility.

Of course, we ought not to refer to the Lord by using cuss words because such words do not apply to Him. They are false in that regard. But neither should we use substitute cuss words like "gosh" or "golly" for God, "gee whiz" for Jesus, "cripes'" for Christ, "heck" for hell, etc. When we use substitute cuss words we are simply trying to circumvent the letter of the Law. People use such substitute cuss words because they think that they are not technically guilty of abusing God's name when they do so. Yet, it is common understanding that the substitute word refers to the thing it substitutes for. People use substitutes to avoid the appearance of violating God's Law. But the intent to swear is still there.

People argue that they didn't technically use God's name, and, therefore, have not violated the letter of the Law. Yet, the reality is that the same motivation drives people to use substitute cuss words every bit as much as to use real cuss words. We are indeed guilty of the spirit of swearing whether real or substitute cuss words are used. All of that pertains to the Third Commandment. As in other areas, Jesus' teaching raises the bar of conformity.

Why is God so concerned about the use of His name? Is it really such a big deal? To understand this we must look at the purpose of swearing. First of all, the very act of swearing implies that the normal use of words is defective. We swear to something to add emphasis to our expression. Everyone knows that people are prone to lying and deceit. So, by swearing we call upon a witness to provide assurance that our word is good, that we are not lying.

"You've gotta believe me. I swear it!"

However, only God can truly witness to such a thing because only God can know our real intentions. Swearing calls attention to our intent. And because only God can know our honest intent, all swearing is really a calling upon Him.

To swear by "heaven's sake" or by "goodness' sake" or "by Jove" (Latin for the ancient god, Jupiter) we are ascribing a power to God's creation that belongs only to God, not to "goodness," nor to "heaven," and certainly not to "Jove." God created the heavens and the earth. God alone is good. God alone is Maker of heaven and earth. To invoke any of other is an act of idolatry.

THE WHOLE TRUTH AND NOTHING BUT THE TRUTH

Yet, all swearing or oath taking is not forbidden. We may swear in court to tell the whole truth and nothing but the truth. But if we fail to rely upon the help of God, we will be unable to honor our oath. Without God's help and active involvement, we will succumb to our sin. Sin cannot be defeated apart from the help and strength of God. Therefore, people can be truly honest only with the help of God, for God is truth itself (Deuteronomy 32:4; Psalms 33:4; John 14:6).

All swearing or taking of oaths must invoke the God of Scripture, who alone is able to witness and assist Christians in the keeping of their oaths, provided the oath gives due glory to God. Consequently, we should be very cautious about taking oaths because their improper use will turn God against us.

The usual source of swearing is disbelief and/or frustration with God. In frustration or anger we shout God's name in defiance. By calling upon a witness to verify our honesty, we admit the need of such a witness, which in turn emphasizes our dishonesty. We are saying in essence, "I am known to lie, but now I call upon a witness to guarantee that I am telling the truth this time." Can an admitted liar be trusted? No. Swearing or oath taking occurs because of our untrustworthiness and inability to keep promises.

The solution to the problem is to be honest in everything. A person who is habitually honest doesn't need to swear because his word is faithful all the time. And, of course, the only way to ensure that our word is faithful is for our thoughts to be faithful. James, following the lead of His Lord and Master, advises Christians to say what they mean and mean what they say. To do less is to subject ourselves to God's judgment.

PRAY

"If you're suffering," says James, "pray" (v. 12).

The word translated *suffering* is the Greek *kakopatheo*. It means to endure hardness, to suffer trouble or affliction. It doesn't simply mean illness, but suggests the trials and tribulations associated with living in this sinful world.

Normally, what happens when people are afflicted is that they respond with frustration, anger, and despair. James, however, advises that Christians not do that. Anger, frustration, and despair are the source of unfaithfulness, swearing, and worse.

"Rather," says James, "pray."

We need to cast all our cares upon Jesus. "When we have a burden, it is surely better to pray for a strong back, rather than to curse the load."[1] Cursing our circumstances, or luck, or the gods, or the Lord Himself not only doesn't do any good, but harms our relationship with God.

Prayer is the remedy for whatever ails you, physical illness, mental illness, stress, trials, tribulations, whatever. We are commanded to pray. But how shall we pray? Most people tell God what they want, and when they don't get it they accuse God of not answering prayer. Then, they think, "Because God doesn't answer prayer, I'm not going to pray. It's just a waste of time."

But we are not to pray for what *we* want. Most of the time we don't even know what we want, and when we think we do, we're usually wrong. Nor do we know what we need to be happy and fulfilled. What we think is essential for our happiness often only serves our selfishness. As Christians we know that the fulfillment of human desires and dreams is often the cause of sin and tragic unhappiness.

Rather, God knows what we need. God knows what is best for us. God knows what will best provide for our maturity and fulfillment. So, as we pray we must learn to pray for what God wants for us. We must learn to simply confess our inadequacies and frustrations to the Lord,

1 Keddie, p. 205.

and allow Him to lead us. We must learn to ask, not just "what would Jesus do?" But "what does God want for me?"

Implicit in such a question is the substitution of God's will for our own. What I want from life is not nearly as important as what God wants for me. Prayer is the perfect opportunity to practice this substitution. In prayer we must learn to confess and obey, rather than demand and expect. The purpose of prayer is not to change God, but to change us. God doesn't change. But we must. We must change our minds and our sinful habits.

The Greek, *kakopatheo*, is both a command and an ongoing action. It doesn't simply mean that we should pray until the problem is resolved. But that we should continue to pray even if the problem isn't resolved—especially when it isn't resolved! Nowhere in Scripture is it suggested that we shouldn't pray when we don't feel like it. Yet, so often I hear Christians say, "I just don't feel like praying." It is precisely when you don't feel like praying that you most need to pray. During those times prayer will be most useful to you.

"Are you suffering? Pray," counsels James. Are you cheerful? Sing—but don't sing just anything, sing psalms, sing praise to God! The Greek word for cheerful is *euthumeo*, which means to be of good cheer, merry, of good courage. It is the joy of life when things are going well.

Unfortunately people tend to ignore God when things are going well. Seldom does anyone say, "I feel so good today, I think I'll pray to the Lord!" People usually turn to God during times of trial and difficulty, and they turn away from God when things are going well. Here James provides a solution to the problem of forgetting God when things are going well—pray. While we are not forbidden to pray at such times, few people actually do.

SING

So James provides an alternative course of action. Since it is natural to sing when you feel good, James suggests singing. Even those who don't sing, will often find themselves with a song in their heart when things are going well. That's the cheerfulness of *euthumeo*.

James suggests that we co-opt this natural joy into the service of the Lord. "Let him sing psalms" (v. 13) interprets a single Greek word, *psalleto*, an imperative verb that commands the singing of psalms! Old Testament Jews were not only characterized by the singing of psalms, but were required to sing psalms. The Lord commands it! If nothing else, read the Psalms with a song in your heart.

But because the book of Psalms was the Old Testament hymnal, the Jews were not only to have a song in their hearts, but actually on their lips as well. The physical act of singing is important to the Lord because the tongue is a window to one's heart. Singing hymns is a spiritual discipline. Have you ever noticed that singing doesn't work, doesn't sound right, unless our hearts are in it. Those who refuse to sing must wrestle with their own disobedience to God's clear command.

How can people ignore or avoid God's commands without neglecting God? People who ignore God's commands also ignore the expression of a heartfelt relationship with God, and can only be hypocrites. A hypocrite is simply a person who says one thing and does another. How can people say they are Christian, say that they love the Lord, and be unwilling to sing praises to Him? You may not sing well —few people do, but to refuse to sing at all is an act of defiance.

To not sing because you don't feel like singing is like not praying because you don't feel like praying. Those are precisely the times in which it is most important for you to be obedient to God. Are Christians free to disobey the Lord because they don't feel like obeying? Hardly! Try telling a policeman that you didn't feel like going the speed limit.

Rather, says Jesus, let your yes be yes and your no be no. We are all called to act out the faith we claim. To do less is to demonstrate a lack of faith. The failure to demonstrate personal faith is the failure to receive God's salvation because salvation is by faith alone. The failure to sing is a serious failure in God's eyes, only because it is a simple command that anyone can obey. "He who is faithful in what is least is faithful also in much; and he who is unjust in what is least is unjust also in much" (Luke 16:10).

If Christ died for you, surely you can sing for Him! Christ suffered to release His people from the punishment for their sins. If we know that, if we have received that release, we will sing, not because we must, but because it is our joy. Our hearts will be filled with thanksgiving and praise to the Lord God Almighty.

CHURCH ORDER

Is anyone among you sick? Let him call for the elders of the church, and let them pray over him, anointing him with oil in the name of the Lord. And the prayer of faith will save the sick, and the Lord will raise him up. And if he has committed sins, he will be forgiven. Confess your trespasses to one another, and pray for one another, that you may be healed. The effective, fervent prayer of a righteous man avails much. Elijah was a man with a nature like ours, and he prayed earnestly that it would not rain; and it did not rain on the land for three years and six months. And he prayed again, and the heaven gave rain, and the earth produced its fruit. —James 5:14-18

The church is to be a hospital for the sick and sinful. Medicine and healing are ministries of the church. The church is for people who have been broken by sin and illness. Jesus said, "Those who are well have no need of a physician, but those who are sick" (Matthew 9:12). The primary confession of the church, that Christ is Lord (Matthew 16:16), must always be fused to the twin confession of one's own sinfulness (1 John 1:8).

James asks, "Is anyone among you sick?" (v. 14). The Greek word is *astheneo*, and means to be weak, feeble, impotent, or powerless. Physical illness will certainly produce such symptoms, but *astheneo* encompasses more than physical illness. The word describes symptoms and is less concerned with their cause than their expression.

The point of the verse is that Christians must call upon the elders to pray for them when they suffer such symptoms. Prayer is not limited to the elders, but James here specifically assigns the responsibility of treating and praying for the sick to the elders. But he also assigns to all Christians the responsibility of calling the elders when they themselves are sick. If the elders are to fulfill their biblical responsibilities, church members must invite them to pray for their needs. If you are ill and fail to call upon the elders for prayer you are undermining the purpose, function, and responsibilities involved in church order.

How Embarrassing

As these words sink in, a glimmer of guilt flashes before us because we have all been ill and not called for the elders. Why have we not called for the elders? There are as many reasons as there are people, but among the most frequent is surely embarrassment. The dictionary says that an embarrassment is, among other things, an obstruction in a stream caused by the lodging of driftwood. The root word means an obstruction or encumberment. Embarrassment is an obstruction in our relationship with God caused by self-consciousness. The root of self-consciousness is, of course, pride. It is self-concern. And illness heightens self-concern.

Fellowship

The reason that so many people ignore the scriptural injunction to call for the elders when they are ill is that people don't really understand or practice genuine Christian fellowship. Fellowship is more than eating together or doing things together. Although such activities are usually part of fellowship, they do not constitute the heart of Christian fellowship. In fact, they miss the most important aspects of Christian fellowship.

Real Christian fellowship is a kind of intimate bearing of one another's burdens, which includes mutual confession of sin and profession of faith. Surely, personal illness is a burden that needs to be shared. The mutual confession of sin is an exercise of humility, and the profession of faith is an exercise of encouragement. Social activity without these essential elements cannot be genuine, fully-orbed, Christian fellowship. Where this kind of genuine fellowship is lacking, it will be difficult to call the elders to pray for you.

However, when you do call the elders to pray for you, don't expect miracles. Elders are not miracle workers. But if they are Godly elders they will be faithful Christians, living on the righteousness of Christ.

Their prayers and service will be effective, fervent, and will "avail much" (v. 16). But that doesn't mean that their prayers or service will always or instantly cure your illness. Nor does it mean that every elder has the particular gifts needed.

Rather, as verse 15 says, "the prayer of faith will save the sick, and the Lord will raise him up." God's purpose in prayer is much wider than simply curing physical illnesses. Illness will always be a part of our fallen life. God, of course, can heal any illness if He so chooses. And sometimes He does, but not always. Physical healing is not guaranteed.

However, there is a promise that is attached to this injunction to call the elders to pray. That promise is verse 15. God promises that the sick who call on the elders will be saved by faith. That doesn't mean that the elders have to be present, or that their salvation will include physical healing. But it does mean that the Lord will raise up the faithful on the last day to a realm without illness or sin.

In the later half of verse 15 James turns his attention to sin. Here James links illness and sin. He may be saying that all illness is the result of sin, which is a biblical truth established at the Fall of Man (Genesis 3). All illness and sin are consequences of the Fall. He is not associating a particular illness with a particular sin. Rather, he associates illness generally with sin generally. Are particular illnesses the result of particular sins? Perhaps, sometimes.

James may be using this verse to invite those who are ill to consider the particular sins that may be associated with their illness. Sometimes an illness can be healed by ceasing a particular sin. Because sin is rampant in this fallen world there are, no doubt, specific sins related to illness. However, it is important that we make the distinction that we are not sinners because we are ill, but we are ill because we are sinners.

Yet, there is a simpler, more probable meaning of this verse. James invites those who are ill to take some time and think about, not only their illness, but their sins. They have an opportunity to do so because they are ill. Their ordinary activities are probably restricted by their illness. Sick people spend time in bed, so James counsels them to make good use of the fact that they are idle, and not waste time feeling sorry for themselves. He counsels them to use the time of their illness to give themselves more completely to God, to confess their sins and profess their faith.

James calls Christians to redeem their time on earth (Ephesians 5:16), even the time of illness. Do not waste time, it is short enough already. Use the time of your illness to grow closer to God in prayer, confession, profession, and praise.

FORGIVENESS

James then adds the assurance that if the ill person "has committed sins, he will be forgiven" (v. 15). Here James addresses the depression and discouragement that often accompanies illness. So, he reminds believers that God's forgiveness is no less available in illness than in health. In fact, he is saying that illness provides a great opportunity in which to take advantage of the prayers of the church as a means to spiritual growth. Things to do when you fall ill include: inviting the elders, considering your sins, confessing your faults, repenting, professing your faith, and confirming your salvation.

Implicit in James' injunction is the right way for a church to order itself. The sick should call for the elders, but so also should those who are sick with sin. When you realize you are sick, call the elders; but also when you realize that sin is crouching at your door. When you have been offended by a fellow Christian, you should prevail upon God's order for the church found in Matthew 18:15-20. When you are offended by a brother, when you disagree with another, when you find yourself angry with someone in the church, your faithfulness depends upon applying God's order to treat the problem. All of these things are also varieties of illness. Being offended, being angry, disagreement among Christians constitute a kind of dis-ease.

Sinful dis-ease should be treated as an illness in the church. Go to that brother and confess your anger or offense or disagreement. If you can't work it out between yourselves privately, then bring another person (usually an elder) to moderate the discussion. If that doesn't resolve it, call in the plurality of elders or the pastor. "Pastoral oversight includes the healing of rifts and arguments."[1] Again, the denial or refusal to engage this process undermines the order of God's church. If you have been offended by another church member, it is *your* responsibility to initiate the amending process—not his. The burden of reconciliation falls to the offended party.

---

1 Keddie, p. 214.

OUR FAULTS

Verse 16 begins, "Confess your trespasses to one another...." The process begins with the confession of one's own sins and trespasses. The King James Version reads, "Confess your *faults* to one another" (italics added). This is to be a general practice, but especially useful when you have been offended by someone. The best way to begin such a discussion is by confessing your own faults, your own sins to the person you need to make amends with.

Again, Scripture counsels that when *you* have been offended by someone it is *your* responsibility to go to that person and confess your own faults to him or her. That is just the opposite of how the world reacts to an offense! To approach another person with a load of accusations always invites trouble. Don't go accusing, go confessing. It will make the difference between a feud and a friend. Again, to fail in this regard is to undermine the order of God's church.

Finally, James provides the example of Elijah as "a man with a nature like ours...who prayed earnestly..." (v. 17). We are not to pray to Elijah as if he were a mediator between God and man—nor to James, but to Christ alone. Elijah only provides an example, as does James and John and Paul and Peter, etc.

Of course, the example of Elijah's effectiveness in prayer often leaves us discouraged because our prayer power doesn't hold a candle to his. But the point isn't that Elijah got what he wanted when he prayed. The point is, rather, that his prayer was perfectly in tune with what God wanted. We are to emulate Elijah's faithfulness because that is all we can do. We can't make our prayers effective. We can't make God give us what we want. All we can do is try to be faithful in conforming our desires to God's desires for us. Our responsibility is to pray, and that's what we must do, and it means conforming our desires for ourselves to God's desire for us.

In faith, then, we can trust in God's salvation and in the testimony of Scripture that He answers prayer. When we find that God is not answering our prayers, we must look to another possibility, other than "God doesn't answer prayer." God does answer faithful prayer, Scripture affirms it. Experience testifies to it. But God doesn't always answer every prayer (Jeremiah 11:11). When He doesn't answer your prayer, the problem does not likely lie with God, but with you. God answers the prayers of the faithful. Is God answering your prayers?

Christ died on the cross so that the prayers of His people would be effective. He died that all of His people might have His righteousness. Christ's righteousness is the only avenue of effective prayer. That righteousness belongs to God's people by faith. Can you claim it? Have you claimed it? Have you been claimed by it?

Reconciliation

Brethren, if anyone among you wanders from the truth, and someone turns him back, let him know that he who turns a sinner from the error of his way will save a soul from death and cover a multitude of sins. —James 5:19-20

We come now to the final two verses of James. In these verses we find an impassioned admonition to practical Christianity. James knows that faith must be practical, that it must be practiced daily in concrete ways, that it is not simply a matter of intellectual detachment, or of an isolated experience or decision.

James' primary theme is reiterated in these last two verses. "Brethren," he said, "if anyone among you wanders from the truth" (v. 19). In our day the whole world is so filled with wanderlust that we ought to read it not "if," but "*when* all of you have wandered from the truth." For the most part our lives, our world, and our thinking are already far from God's truth. The words "if any" suggest that the majority of the people will not wander from God's truth. But the reality of our world is that our contemporary churches have wandered too far already. The state or condition of God's church today surely testifies to our wanderlust.

However, the realization of the truth of this fact provides no justification for pointing the finger at others to assuage our own guilt. Certainly others have been involved in tempting us away from the Lord, but our sin is not somebody else's fault. Sin is rampant. We cannot escape its perversion. We cannot ignore it, nor can we get completely free from it this side of glory. Human sin has become a modern media event. It is published widely in print and piped into our homes electronically. Yet, if the truth be known, we enjoy it. People sin because they like it.

We have all been deeply affected by the wholesale cultural rejection of God that has advanced over the past thirty—or fifty, or two-hundred years, or whatever. The point is that our normal patterns of thinking and living today are not based upon God's Word. We are products of our society—our faith has already been significantly reshaped by the forces of modernism. We are already much farther down the pike than most people care to realize.

And for the most part people don't realize it. To try to call attention to our present situation is like trying to get a fish to notice the water. It's invisible. It supports him. He lives in it. He breathes it and eats it. It's everywhere. He cannot live without it, but he's not aware of it. That's how sin is to us. We live in sin like fish live in water.

James wrote, not to the modern age, but to Christians who had not yet wandered so far into such polluted waters. He wrote to warn Christians of the dangers of getting lost in faulty thinking. For the most part, we can only make sense of James if we read him, not as warning us of a potential danger, but as providing historical perspective on a danger into which we have already fallen. By reading James this way we might be able to discern the place from which Christianity itself has fallen, and, thereby, find our way home. All of this is to say that we are already far deeper into the polluted waters of sin than we think we are.

The waters that James warned Christians not to enter, were entered some time ago by our society and by our churches as we came into the Modern era—and perhaps much earlier. Like the Fall of Adam, we have been born into sin, born into a particular historical momentum. History does not run backwards, so we cannot return to some premodern Christian version of Eden. We are so far gone that we can look back upon the historical wreckage of many modern utopian dreams, some ostensibly Christian, some not. However, we are not so far gone that we cannot take an accurate reading of our own current historical bearings. We can and we must evaluate the extent of our own wandering from God's truth. And that evaluation begins with the acknowledgment of our own personal sin and culpability in sin.

As we do that we must clearly and intentionally recommit ourselves, individually and corporately, to return—not to the past splendor of some historical moment, real or imagined, but to God Himself. What

James says here about those who have wandered from God's truth applies to us all. This is the practical application of God's Word for our everyday lives. May we give ourselves to it wholeheartedly.

REPENTANCE

The gist of these final few verses is repentance and reconciliation. Repentance and reconciliation are like two sides of a single coin. Like love and marriage, they function best when they function together. And like marriage, repentance and reconciliation take work. They don't just happen. The difficulty with repentance and reconciliation is that engaging them forces us to admit that we have been wrong. And that's difficult. People don't like to be wrong. It's embarrassing—especially for Christians. Even more so for contemporary Christians.

Its difficult for Christians to say, "Yep, I've been a Christian for X many years (fill in a number), but I've never really gotten it right."

"So, what good is being a Christian if you still don't have it right after so many years? Why bother? I can get it wrong without all the work, the guilt, and the trouble," the world answers. And, indeed, they can and do.

The reason that such a Christian doesn't have it right, is that being a Christian isn't really about having it right. It's about admitting that we've got it wrong, and can't get it right without Christ. It is Christ who's got it right. Our responsibility is to admit that we have gotten it wrong. I'm not saying that being a Christian doesn't improve personal morality. It most certainly does. But mere moral improvement does not a Christian make. Like history, Gospel logic flows one direction, but not the other.

Christianity is first and foremost about repentance. It begins in repentance or it doesn't begin at all. And the problem with repentance is that it is embarrassing. People naturally resist it. People don't like it and they don't want to do it—and they surely don't want to do it publicly. "What would people think if I confessed all that stuff, and admitted that I have been fooling myself and my loved ones?"

Church leaders think, "If I call attention to someone's sin, someone might call attention to mine. So, I'll just keep quiet. I certainly don't want my laundry aired publicly—especially since I'm a leader. It would make the church look bad. So, I won't say anything." The result is that without a concerted effort to address sin, theological error, and false belief in the church, these very things find a welcome climate and grow profusely in God's church.

It is not that Christians are to point the finger and judge those who have erred from God's truth. Nobody wants to be accused. But neither are Christians to ignore sin, theological error, and false belief. These things are clearly wrong according to Scripture. Rather, the purpose of Christianity is reconciliation, to bring back to the Lord those who have strayed. If we start accusing and pointing fingers, we'll just make people mad. That's precisely what Satan wants.

But, on the other hand, if we pretend that there aren't any of these things in the church and that no one is ever wrong, we will be untrue to God's Word. So, we must hold on to God's truth, even when it embarrasses people and makes them mad. But why do people get mad about God's truth? Because people think that repentance makes them look foolish because their pride refuses to admit to error and weakness. And because Christianity is social—public, it makes them look foolish publicly.

RECONCILIATION

There were once two brothers who got into a quarrel. The most serious fights are always between family members. These two brothers separated, promising never to speak to one another again. Their mother did all she could to reconcile them, but to no avail. The feud persisted. It greatly distressed the mother and she lost all sense of peace and happiness. It troubled her so much that she couldn't sleep, and she began to lose weight.

One brother saw how much his mother was affected, and bought her a gift to try to make her feel better. But she refused to take it.

"I don't want any gift from you until you reconcile with your brother," she scolded.

That's how God feels as well. We can't worship rightly until and unless we resolve all our hard feelings, our grudges, and anger toward others. As long as we are unreconciled with one another, our worship won't be right, our personal faith won't be right, our families won't be right, our church won't be right, etc. Is it any wonder that the world and God's church is as it is?

Christ has provided the reconciliation that is required by God. In Christ we are already reconciled before God. For ages the world hoped for Christ. The Old Testament prophets and saints hoped and prayed for His coming. They knew that He would do for us what we cannot do for ourselves. And indeed Christ has done it. Two thousand years ago, He completed the necessary atonement for the sins of His people.

But now we come before God in worship and Jesus says,

> "if you bring your gift to the altar, and there remember that your
> brother has something against you, leave your gift there before
> the altar, and go your way. First be reconciled to your brother,
> and then come and offer your gift" (Matthew 5:22-24).

In verse 19 James tells us that real ministry begins in the church. It begins with other Christians, and particularly, with other members of our own church. We have to straighten ourselves out before we can help others get straight. Our own homes are the neglected fields of biblical application. It is an interesting fact that one of the greatest mission fields in the world exists in America. That includes our own churches and families. The reason for this dire situation is that Christian churches and families have failed to heed God's Word themselves. This is not an accusation, but a confession!

How can someone go off and minister among the lost, when his own household is a spiritual mess? He can't. How can Christians minister in the inner city when their own churches are in spiritual shambles? They can't. They can go, but they can't help because they don't have the experience or the knowledge that is needed to really help others. That experience and knowledge is gained at home.

How can we invite lost sinners into our fellowship, when our fellowship is full of feuds, superficial commitments, and immature beliefs? What do we have to offer the lost? They already have plenty of feuds and superficialities of their own. They know all too well the problems of superficial commitment and immature belief. Those outside the church can see it for what it is better than those inside. And they want nothing to do with it!

Before we can successfully reach out to others, we must get our own house in order. One of the most serious problems we face today is that many Christians and churches are prematurely concerned with evangelism. They want to help others do what they have not done themselves. Contrary to popular opinion evangelism is not the first priority of the church. Worship is the first priority of the church. And Jesus said that we can't even worship rightly unless and until we first reconcile with our brothers.

Too many Christians want to share God's truth before they rightly understand it themselves. Have you ever noticed that people get ahold of a piece of God's truth and immediately try to share it. But because it is only a piece of the truth, half of the truth, it only half communicates. People get a genuine insight about some doctrine or other and try to cram it down someone's throat, thinking that they are helping to "save" them, when all they are doing is driving them away from Christ.

God's truth is about much more than mere doctrine. Doctrine is important, but it isn't just some abstract idea. Biblical doctrine is always fused to biblical practice. What is missing in the contemporary churches is actual biblical practice. Errors in thinking produce errors in practice. Following the wrong map cannot lead to the right destination. Following the wrong recipe will not produce the right cake. Similarly, if you have the right map but do not travel, you will not get to the right destination either. Nor if you have the right recipe but do not bake, you will not have any cake. Biblical doctrine and biblical practice have been torn asunder and must be reunited. As we consider how best to do that we must realize that action follows thought. Action, behavior, deeds, works begin in thoughts and intentions.

Take smoking as an example. Smoking begins with the idea to smoke, so we can say that faulty thinking results in the practice of smoking. But once it begins, the smoking itself begins to effect how people think. Logic and reason are twisted as they engage and then rationalize their addictive behavior.

Smoking is a habit. People don't smoke because they believe that it will cause lung cancer and heart disease. Those things are true, but smokers rationalize them away. They know certain things are true, but they don't live on the basis of that truth. The forces of habituation overpower their ability to make intelligent choices. The error of not living by the truth that smokers know results in all kinds of ill effects in their lives. So it is with biblical truth.

James calls for brothers and sisters in the Lord to care for one another in this regard. We are to help each other when we see each other wandering from God's Word. But we are to do so according to God's established pattern of authority. There is a fine line between meddling in some else's life and providing needed spiritual care. God's Word respects that line. We cannot deny our responsibility to help, but we must do all we can to ensure that our help is actually helpful.

The most helpful thing that we can do for others is to ensure that our own lives and our own church are governed according to God's Word. To simply do that would likely clear up eighty percent of this world's troubles. So, lets begin there. Let's live on the basis of what we know. Let's govern ourselves and our churches by the Book in the light of Christ and God's grace.

But let's not do it harshly or rashly. Rather, let us commit ourselves to follow God's Word regarding church order and discipline, always with a desire for reconciliation and restoration, and always making use of the cloak of love because love covers a multitude of sins.

Can we do that? Is that even possible?

It is, but only by God's grace and in God's time. We cannot make it happen. But we can make ourselves available to it.

SCRIPTURE INDEX

Made in the
USA
Lexington, KY